POLICY AND PRACTICE IN HEALTH AND SOCIAL CARE
NUMBER SEVEN

Learning Disability and Social Inclusion

POLICY AND PRACTICE IN HEALTH AND SOCIAL CARE

1: Jacqueline Atkinson, *Private and Public Protection: Civil Mental Health Legislation* (2006)

2: Charlotte Pearson (ed.), *Direct Payments and Personalisation of Care* (2006)

3: Joyce Cavaye, *Hidden Carers* (2006)

4: Mo McPhail (ed.), *Service User and Carer Involvement: Beyond Good Intentions* (2007)

5: Anne Stafford and Sharon Vincent (eds), *Safeguarding and Protecting Children and Young People* (2008)

6: Alison Petch, *Health and Social Care: Establishing a Joint Future?* (2007)

7: Gillian McIntyre, *Learning Disability and Social Inclusion* (2008)

8: Ailsa Cook, *Dementia and Well-being: Possibilities and Challenge* (2008)

9: Michele Burman and Jenny Johnstone, *Youth Justice* (2008)

POLICY AND PRACTICE IN HEALTH AND SOCIAL CARE

SERIES EDITORS

JOYCE CAVAYE and ALISON PETCH

Learning Disability and Social Inclusion

A review of current policy and practice

Dr Gillian MacIntyre

Lecturer, Glasgow School of Social Work, University of Strathclyde, Glasgow

DUNEDIN

Published by
Dunedin Academic Press Ltd
Hudson House
8 Albany Street
Edinburgh EH1 3QB
Scotland

ISBN: 978-1-903765-83-8
ISSN 1750-1407

British Library Cataloguing in Publication data
A catalogue record for this book is available from the British Library

Typeset by Makar Publishing Production
Printed and bound in Great Britain by CPod

Contents

Series Editors' Introduction

Recent years have witnessed a strong policy drive to achieve equal citizenship for individuals with learning disabilities. The importance of recognising people's rights to choice and control about different aspects of their life and of raising expectations of a good quality of life have been highlighted for Scotland in The same as you? and for England in Valuing People.

Achieving some of the policy aspirations in practice has proved difficult, not least in the tricky area of social inclusion. This volume offers a sober analysis of the extent to which emerging practice has been able to achieve greater inclusion for people with learning disabilities, most particularly in the fields of training, employment, health and well-being. The assumption that paid employment is always the most appropriate goal is questioned, and the poor performance of health services in respect of people with learning disabilities is highlighted. The tension between inclusion and the provision of specialist services is explored, together with the potential of local area co-ordination; a model developed in Australia which has only been adopted in Scotland to date in the UK.

At the heart of the debate is the nature of the support networks available to each individual, regardless of their disability. To what extent are these networks based on informal friendships and supports? To what extent are they constructed through input from formal professional supports? And can one promote the other, for example friendship networks emerging from more functional support. Most importantly to what extent are different forms of support networks associated with greater or lesser social inclusion? Not all these questions can yet be answered, but this volume provides an excellent summary both of the available evidence and of the central challenges.

Dr Joyce Cavaye
Faculty of Health and Social Care, The Open University in Scotland, Edinburgh

Professor Alison Petch
Director, ***research in practice*** **for adults***, Dartington Hall Trust, Totnes, Devon*

Glossary of Abbreviations

AGN	Adult Guidance Networks
ASN	Additional Support Needs
ASN Act	Additional Support for Learning (Scotland) Act (the)
DDA	Disability Discrimination Act 1995
DST	Disability Service Team
EBP	Education Business Partnerships
ESB	Emotional, Social and Behavioural Problems
FNA	Future Needs Assessment
IB	Incapacity Benefit
IEP	Individual Education Plans
LEC	Local Enterprise Companies
LLP	Local Learning Partnerships
MLD	Moderate Learning Disability
NDDP	New Deal for Disabled People
NEET	Not in Education, Employment or Training
PA	Adult Personal Assistants
PAM	Professions Allied to Medicine
PSPS	Post-School Psychological Service
SEETLLD	Scottish Executive Enterprise, Transport and Lifelong Learning Department
SEN	Special Educational Needs

Chapter 1

Setting the Scene: Key Trends in Policy Development

People with learning disabilities in Scotland and across the UK have been the target of considerable legislative and policy changes over recent years. Relevant policy developments straddle a number of key areas. These include education policy, learning disability policy and services, welfare to work policies, the social inclusion and social justice agenda and anti-discrimination legislation. A key theme relates to the inclusion of people with learning disabilities in the community – in education, training and employment and in relation to accessing health, housing and leisure services. This reflects part of a wider government drive to promote social inclusion and encourage participation based on the rights and obligations of citizenship. This is perhaps best exemplified by the review of learning disability services, *The Same As You?*, published by the Scottish Executive in 2000, and the parallel document in England, *Valuing People*, which was published by the Department of Health in 2001. As a result of these changes, people with learning disabilities, their families, service providers, policy makers and other professionals working alongside them have to negotiate their way through a complex array of services.

The aim of this book is to address this complexity by mapping and critically reviewing relevant policy developments, particularly in Scotland but across the UK as a whole. Drawing on the available research evidence, the book adopts a life-cycle approach, tracing the journey taken by people with learning disabilities upon leaving school and making the transition to adulthood and beyond. Focusing on the major areas identified in *The Same As You?* (Scottish Executive, 2000a), the book identifies key messages in the fields of education, training and employment, health and social work. This introductory chapter highlights key trends in policy development and illustrates the ways in which these policies have been influenced by theoretical perspectives such as the social model of disability and theories of citizenship.

Defining learning disability

There is currently no nationally agreed definition of what constitutes a 'learning disability'. The terminology used varies according to the context, although the term 'learning disability' is used throughout this book. Other common terminology currently in use includes 'learning difficulty', while in the American literature the terms 'intellectual impairment', 'intellectual disability' and 'mental retardation' are widely used. 'Learning disability' and 'learning difficulty' are often used interchangeably although some disability writers have expressed a preference for the term 'learning difficulty' (see, for example, Chappell, 1992,1997; Goodley, 2001a, 2001b), which they perhaps regard as having less negative connotations. The term 'learning disability' has been adopted here in order to maintain consistency with much of the British writing in the field. In addition, the majority of policy documents and service provision within the UK use the term 'learning disability', so using the term here avoids confusion.

Defining what constitutes a learning disability brings further confusion (see Diesfield, 1999; Klotz, 2001; Ho, 2004). It has been noted in the literature that the concept of learning disability is relatively difficult to define and there are many different definitions currently in use. Some of the more medicalised definitions continue to rely on IQ testing. Other definitions take a more functional approach, focusing on areas of difficulty in comparison with the general population. According to Diesfield (1999, p. 23):

> 'Learning disability' is not an absolute term but a socially relative one and it reflects an expectation of those mental capacities which are required for 'normal functioning' in society. Therefore, labelling people as 'handicapped' is an indicator of what can be tolerated in mainstream settings.

In a consultation document issued by the Department for Education and Skills in 2002, new categories and definitions of special educational needs were introduced to aid planning and policy development. 'Moderate learning difficulty', for example, was described as:

> developmental delay across a number of areas. Pupils with moderate learning difficulty will have attainments below expected levels in most subjects in the curriculum. Pupils have difficulty in acquiring basic literacy and numeracy skills and in many cases will have speech and language difficulties associated with intellectual delay. A few may also have low self esteem, low levels of concentration, under-developed social skills and have behavioural, emotional and social difficulty and/or physical disability that affect their learning abilities. (Department for Education and Skills, 2002, p. 8)

In the response to the consultation, there were a number of concerns that the description of moderate learning disability (MLD) was too broad.

However, according to the Department for Education and Skills (2002) it remains the most difficult description to give a clear boundary to. Indeed, Higgins *et al.* (2002) argued that the formal definition of what constitutes a learning disability is in constant flux. They suggested that the definition changes according to evolving legislation and other eligibility requirements (see also Ho, 2004). The difficulty, according to Riddell and Banks (2001), arises when policy makers have used different definitions of learning disability and so are talking about different populations, thus leading to confusion (see also Mabbett, 2005).

The definition of learning disability adopted by the Scottish Executive within *The Same As You*? (Scottish Executive, 2000a) takes account of the diverse nature of learning disability and focuses on individual need. It is defined as:

> a significant lifelong condition which has three facets:
>
> - reduced ability to understand new or complex information or to learn new skills
> - reduced ability to cope independently
> - a condition which started before adulthood (before the age of 18) with a lasting effect on the individuals development.
>
> (Scottish Executive, 2000a, p. 103)

A statistical release from the Scottish Executive suggests that in 2006 there were an estimated 22, 859 adults with learning disabilities known to local authorities across Scotland. This corresponds to approximately 5.5 adults with learning disabilities per 1,000 of the population generally (Scottish Executive, 2007a). The majority of adults with learning disabilities (57%) were male. Thirty-one per cent were aged between 35 and 49 and this equates to 6.1 per 1,000 of the general population in that age group. Among 18–20-year-olds, 1,750 had a learning disability. This represents 8.5 per 1,000 population of this age group (Scottish Executive, 2007a).

Relevant policy developments in the field of learning disability

This book is written at a time of changing expectations with regard to the lives of people with learning disabilities. These changing expectations have occurred at all levels – among policy makers, service providers, professionals, family members of people with learning disabilities and people with learning disabilities themselves. Policy developments that are of relevance to the lives of people with learning disabilities sit alongside these changing expectations as to what are appropriate and acceptable life choices and experiences for this group. Broadly, people with learning disabilities are no longer viewed as objects of fear and ridicule who should be segregated in long-stay institutions as exemplified by the 1913 Lunacy Act. People with learning disabilities are increasingly living within local communities as a result of policies of de-institutionalisation, which gained momentum after the introduction of the NHS and Community Care Act in 1990 (Cattermole *et al.*, 1990; Stalker and Hunter, 1999; Forrester-Jones *et al.*, 2002). People with learning disabilities have an increasing presence in the community as a consequence of not only de-institutionalisation but also policies at a local level to reconfigure day services. These are increasingly shifting from the world of the day centre or adult resource centre into the community. There is a growing expectation that people with learning disabilities should increasingly be able to participate in the worlds of further education, training and employment. They should be able to enjoy improved health and well-being, living as independently as possible while making use of community resources such as leisure opportunities.

In recent years, perhaps the best exemplar of a policy development which highlights these changing expectations towards people with learning disabilities is *The Same As You*?, published by the Scottish Executive in 2000. This national review of learning disability services in Scotland looked in depth at current provision in relation to health and social care services as well as at education, employment and other day opportunities. The key focus of the review was on lifestyles and the key principle was that people with learning disabilities should be able to lead normal lives. A series of goals was set out that suggested that people with learning disabilities should be able to:

- be included;
- be better understood and supported by the communities in which they live;
- have information about their needs and services available so they can take part in decisions about them;
- be at the centre of decision-making and have more control over their care;
- have the same opportunities as others to get a job, develop as individuals, spend time with family and friends, enjoy life and get the extra support they need to do this;
- use local services where possible and special services if they need them.

To these ends the review recommended changes in a number of areas. It recommended that local authorities and health boards should draw up Partnership in Practice agreements by 2001. These agreements were to include plans to ensure that there were needs assessments for young people who were planning to leave school and would need to use adult services, as well as plans for developing and commissioning accommodation and social support. The review also recommended the introduction of local area co-ordinators, whose role would be to co-ordinate services and provide information, provide support for families and organise funding. The local area co-ordinator would also be responsible for producing Personal Life Plans for all adults with learning disabilities (who wanted one). These plans would aid long-term planning and would replace community care assessments. The plan would describe how the person with learning disabilities, their family and professionals would work together to help the person lead a fuller life. It was recommended that everyone who wanted a plan should have one (Scottish Executive, 2000b). A Scottish Executive statistical release in 2007 shows progress that has been made to date in each of these areas. In 2006, a local area co-ordination service was provided by 28 of the 32 local authorities in Scotland (Scottish Executive, 2007a). This had risen from 12 in 2003 (Scottish Executive, 2005a). In addition, 29% of adults known to local authorities had a personal life plan or person-centred plan (Scottish Executive, 2007a).

The review was comprehensive and far-reaching and examined service provision in respect of all areas of the lives of people with learning disabilities. A number of areas were prioritised, however. One of the key themes of the review was to improve employment opportunities for people with learning disabilities. It recommended that local authorities should place more emphasis on developing employment services for people with learning disabilities and it demonstrated that this could be cost-effective.

Such was the commitment of the Scottish Executive to supporting people with learning disabilities to move into employment that a short-life working group was set up to look at the issues around employment in more depth. The working group identified a number of barriers that will be discussed in more depth in the next chapter. In 2006, only 16% of adults with a learning disability known to local authorities in Scotland engaged in some form of employment, and only 29% of this group were in open employment – this corresponds to around 5% of all adults with learning disabilities (Scottish Executive, 2007a).

Working groups were also formed to look in more depth at de-institutionalisation, local area co-ordination, day services and advocacy. The subgroup on local area co-ordination published its recommendations in 2002. Local area co-ordination will be discussed in more depth in Chapter 5. The report on the closure of long-stay hospitals entitled *Home at Last?* (Scottish Executive, 2004a) suggested that considerable progress had been made in relation to resettlement. By January 2003 the number of hospital places in Scotland had been reduced to 900, with another 652 discharges planned by 2005. The group made a number of recommendations based on a set of core principles. These principles suggested that beyond 2005, no one with a learning disability should live in or receive their short breaks in a hospital setting. In addition people with learning disabilities and their families should have been as closely involved in the process as possible, with adequate support mechanisms available within the community (Scottish Executive, 2004a). It is beyond the scope of this book to look in depth at housing, but Petch *et al.* (2000) produced a report that explored in depth the experiences of people with learning disabilities moving into local communities as a result of the hospital resettlement programme in Scotland.

The subgroup that looked at day opportunities identified a number of key themes which they suggested should influence the development of day services over the next decade. As part of their remit they spoke to a range of people with learning disabilities, their families and staff members. As a result of these discussions they found a need for varied and flexible services that offer a range of opportunities. They found that people with learning disabilities wanted to be included in and make a positive contribution to their local communities, with purposeful activities that might lead to employment. In addition, they suggested a person-centred approach, involving service users and their families in the running of services – thus ensuring a partnership approach (Scottish Executive, 2006a). Each of these key themes will be returned to throughout the course of this book.

The final subgroup of relevance looked at the provision of advocacy services for people with learning disabilities, their families and people with autistic spectrum disorders (Scottish Executive, 2006b). The report set out a number of action points and recommendations in order to improve the quality and accessibility of advocacy to people of all ages in Scotland. It identified 28 action points. These related largely to raising awareness and sharing information to ensure people were aware of the types of advocacy available and the kinds of services these can offer. Local authority areas were to develop 'local advocacy plans' that stated how people could get advocacy support on a range of issues including housing, transport and employment (Scottish Executive, 2006b). Further research is required that looks in depth at the impact of advocacy services on the lives of people with learning disabilities in Scotland and across the UK as a whole.

In England, a similar process took place with the publication of the White Paper *Valuing People* in 2001 (Department of Health, 2001) – the first White Paper published on the lives of people with learning disabilities in over 30 years. In a similar way to *The Same As You*? (Scottish Executive, 2000a), people with learning disabilities, their families, carers and other organisations were involved in gathering and producing the information. *Valuing People* is based on the principles that people with learning disabilities have the right to citizenship, inclusion in their local communities, choice in daily life and real chances to be independent.

Again these principles relate to the themes that run through this book and will be explored in depth throughout the remaining chapters.

In 2005, a review was commissioned to examine progress made in relation to *Valuing People* and to identify future priorities (Department of Health, 2005). The review found many examples of good practice that related to person-centred planning, Supporting People, direct payments and partnership working. Implementation was patchy, however, and varied by geographical area. People with learning disabilities from Black and Minority Ethnic Communities appeared to be particularly disadvantaged. Although there was increasing recognition of the rights of people with learning disabilities to be active and valued citizens, it was recognised that more work was needed. To this end, five priority areas were identified. These were about improving health inequalities for people with learning disabilities, helping people to get paid employment, making sure people have more housing choices, stopping people being sent away from their local communities and, finally, making the transition to adulthood a positive experience (Valuing People Support Team, 2005). Again, key messages in relation to several of these areas will be discussed in greater detail during the rest of this book.

Changing structures of support

Key policy developments have resulted in a period of rapid change and development in service provision in the fields of education, training and employment, health and social work. Each of these areas will be addressed in turn in the remainder of the book. It is useful at this point to identify and summarise some of the key changes that have occurred, in order to familiarise the reader with the context. The development of policies and services has been complicated further by the onset of devolution arising after the Scotland Act 1998. The Scottish Parliament has been given devolved responsibility for many key areas including lifelong learning and special educational needs. Even prior to the onset of devolution, there were growing differences in special educational needs policies north and south of the border (Riddell *et al.*, 2000; Riddell and Banks, 2001; Riddell *et al.* 2002; Riddell, 2004). The Westminster Parliament has reserved responsibility for other areas of significance such as the benefits system, welfare to work policies and anti-discrimination legislation.

Changes in education and careers guidance

The Same As You? (Scottish Executive, 2000a) recommended that where possible young people with learning disabilities should be educated alongside their non-disabled peers in mainstream settings, with additional support where necessary. The movement towards education for all young people in mainstream settings gained momentum in the late 1990s and is exemplified in the Standards in Scotland's Schools etc. Act 2000 as well as the more recent Education (Additional Support for Learning) (Scotland) Act 2004. The most recent figures from the Scottish Executive suggest that in 2006, 36,148 pupils (5.1%) had a co-ordinated support plan or Individualised Educational Programme, or had provision levels set by a record of needs (7.1% of boys and 3.2% of girls). About 1.5% of pupils had a moderate to profound learning disability and 1% had a specific learning difficulty in language or maths, such as dyslexia. Most of them (29,173, or 81%) are in mainstream schools. They make up 4.2% of mainstream school pupils. There is some difficulty in comparing the figures with those from previous years, given the recent introduction of the Education (Additional Support for Learning) (Scotland) Act in 2004 and the resultant changes in categories and definitions. The table below should, however, give some idea of changes that have occurred in recent years (Scottish Executive, 2006c).

Table 1.1 Pupils with Additional Support Needs

	All time in mainstream classes		Some time in mainstream classes		Mainstream school, but non-mainstream classes		Special school	
	Number	*%*	*Number*	*%*	*Number*	*%*	*Number*	*%*
2003	18,838	61	3,747	12	681	2	7,573	25
2004	20,999	64	3,612	11	752	2	7,242	22
2005	22,788	66	3,879	11	873	3	7,037	20
2006	24,195	67	4,394	12	584	2	6,975	19

Further caution is required when interpreting these figures because since 2006, all reasons for additional support have been included, rather than just a pupil's main difficulty in learning. This has led to an increase in the reported incidence of each difficulty. While this change has only been partly implemented so far, the figures now represent a more accurate picture of incidence.

Upon leaving school, it is likely that the majority of young people who have been classified as having a learning disability will go on to some form of further education course. Data is not readily available on the destinations of young people leaving special schools and on those young people with a record of needs leaving mainstream schools. At a national level, school leaver destinations are not broken down by additional support needs. At a local level, however, figures from Glasgow City Council suggest that in 2001, 50% of those young people leaving a special school in Glasgow went on to study at a college of further education (Glasgow City Council, 2001). Fourteen per cent went on to a training placement, 14% became unemployed and 6% moved into employment. The destinations of leavers from Scottish schools (Scottish Executive, 2006c) are not broken down by additional support need but nonetheless offer some point of comparison. In 2001/02, 32% of Scottish school leavers moved on to higher education, 20% went on to full-time further education, 6% went on to a training programme and 23% obtained employment. Those who became NEET (not in education, employment or training) totalled 16% (Scottish Executive, 2006c).

The Further and Higher Education (Scotland) Act 1992 placed a duty on the Secretary of State for Scotland to secure the adequate and efficient provision of further education in Scotland. In doing so he was to 'have regard to the requirements of persons over school age with learning difficulties', which was used in a broad sense to include difficulties in learning and barriers to learning (Scottish Executive, 2000b). To encourage this, colleges were to receive an enhanced payment for students with disabilities. This additional weighting for disabled students was further enhanced if they participated in a special needs course (often a two-year course referred to as an extension or development course) as opposed to a mainstream course. As a result, disabled students, particularly those with less intensive support needs, became financially attractive to further education colleges and a range of courses to attract these students were developed.

During their time at school or further education and upon leaving these environments, young people with learning disabilities are likely to require the guidance of a careers advisor. In Scotland, this guidance was traditionally provided by careers service companies that covered local areas within Scotland, resulting in discrepancies across the country in terms of service provision. The White Paper *A Smart, Successful Scotland: Ambitions for the Enterprise Networks* (Scottish Executive, 2000b) laid out the plans to develop Careers Scotland as part of an attempt to reduce unemployment and narrow the gap in terms of inequalities. Careers Scotland was developed as a national agency aligning the Careers Service, Education Business Partnerships (EBPs), Adult Guidance Networks (AGNs) and Local Learning Partnerships (LLPs) with Scottish Enterprise and Highlands and Islands Enterprise (Riddell, 2004). The new agency became operational in April 2002. Careers Scotland now has responsibility for managing the 'all age guidance projects' and the 'inclusiveness projects' funded as a result of the recommendations of the Beattie committee (Scottish Executive, 1999a) (which will be discussed in greater detail in Chapter 2). Careers Scotland is also responsible for managing Get Ready for Work, a training programme for 16- and 17-year-olds with additional support needs, which replaced the Special Needs Skillseekers Programme (this will be discussed in greater detail in Chapter 3).

Parallel developments in careers guidance in the rest of the UK took the form of the introduction of the Connexions service, which was responsible for all young people aged 13 to 19 in England and Wales, giving particular priority to those young people at greatest risk of not making a 'successful' transition to adulthood (Department for Education and Skills, 2001). The service is currently under review as a result of the publication of the Green Paper *Youth Matters* in 2005 (Department for Education and Skills, 2005), which acknowledged that services did not always meet the needs of all young people or work together as effectively as they should. The aim is now to integrate Connexions with a wider range of services at local level while retaining the Connexions brand.

Changes in training and employment services

As mentioned above, the review of learning disability services placed particular importance on creating and finding employment opportunities for people with learning disabilities. It is therefore important to note than in addition to the changes that have occurred in relation to careers guidance, changes have occurred at a UK-wide level to the services provided by the Employment Service and the Benefits Agency. Again, these changes are particularly relevant for people with a range of impairments of all ages who wish to enter or move closer to the labour market. The Green Paper *New Ambitions for Our Country: A New Contract for Welfare* (Department of Social Security, 1998), which produced the now infamous statement 'work for those who can, security for those who cannot', aimed to remove barriers to work for disabled people.

One result of the recommendations made was the creation of Jobcentre Plus, a new agency that brought together the existing Jobcentre and Benefits Agency under one roof. Between October 2001 and January 2002, 56 pathfinder offices were established. By October 2002 further Jobcentre Plus offices had opened, and the network was due to be completed by October 2006 (Riddell *et al.*, 2005). Alongside the creation of the new agency was the introduction of new terms and conditions for benefit claimants. All new benefit claimants now have to attend an initial work-focused interview in order to assist them to overcome any initial barriers to work.

Recent proposed changes focusing on those claiming Incapacity Benefit (IB) have been outlined in the consultation document *A New Deal for Welfare: Empowering People to Work* (Department for Work and Pensions, 2006). The aim is to reform both the benefits system and the ways in which people are supported back to work by reducing by one million the number on incapacity benefits, helping 300,000 lone parents into work and increasing by one million the number of older workers.

Jobcentre Plus continues to provide a range of employment programmes geared towards the needs of disabled people, including the New Deal for Disabled People and the Work Preparation Programme. The role of frontline Jobcentre Plus staff has become increasingly focused on providing assessment and guidance, and a relatively small amount of time is spent liaising with employers and offering support to disabled people in the field (Riddell, 2004).

The restructuring of these services may be seen as part of an overall plan to rationalise services in order to make best use of resources. The reorganisation of the Careers Service is part of an attempt to provide more equitable services across the country. In addition, the changes to the structure of the employment and benefits agencies represent an attempt to smooth the transition from inactivity to employment, hence removing some of the barriers faced by disabled people seeking work. On the other hand, as with the introduction of any new service, the changes have introduced an element of confusion felt by service users and staff alike. The infancy of the services needs to be borne in mind when considering the experiences of people with learning disabilities.

Changes within health services

People with learning disabilities have a range of health needs associated with their particular conditions or syndromes as well as general health needs which are similar to those of the rest of the population. As with education, training and employment, the review of learning disability services in Scotland recommended that people with learning disabilities should have their health needs met in mainstream settings where possible, accessing specialist services where this was necessary. Across the country a range of approaches to meeting the health care needs of people with learning disabilities have been adopted. An ongoing debate relates to the use of specialist or generic health care workers. In addition, greater use has been made of preventative approaches to the health care of this group in recent years with, for instance, the introduction of health checks (see, for example, Curtice *et al.*, 2001a, 2001b; Curtice and Long, 2002). These areas will be discussed in greater detail in Chapter 4.

Changes within social work

The review of learning disability services recognised the importance of the social worker's role in the lives of people with learning disabilities living in the community. In particular social workers had a key role to play in terms of assisting people to access services. Alongside this, the review recommended the introduction of local area co-ordinators as outlined above. This is discussed in greater detail in Chapter 5. Sitting alongside the review of learning disability services, social work in Scotland has undergone a series of changes as a result of *Changing Lives: Report of the 21st Century Review of Social Work* published by the Scottish Executive (2006d).

The review took place after a series of incidents where social workers were negatively implicated. The review recognised that the situation could not continue unchanged and made a series of recommendations in relation to the role of the social worker in 21st century Scotland. Of particular relevance here was the increased emphasis on joint working with other professionals as well as the move towards personalised budgets and self-directed care, both of which were emphasised in *The Same As You*? (Scottish Executive, 2000a). The Scottish Executive evidenced their commitment to personalised budgets and self-directed care in a directive published in 2007 (Scottish Executive, 2007b). This move is likely to have implications for people with learning disabilities in terms of both the modes of delivery and types of services they can expect to receive. These areas are discussed in greater detail in Chapter 5.

Concepts that have influenced policy development and service provision

The aim of this first introductory chapter has been to present to the reader at a glance the four broad areas – education; training and employment; health; social work – that will be discussed in depth throughout the rest of the book. In order to understand the context it was important to firstly outline key aspects of policy development and change in relation to each of these areas. Within each of the four areas it is possible to identify three key concepts that have influenced the development of policy. These concepts, or themes, will run through the remainder of this book.

Social inclusion

One of the key questions which this book seeks to address is the extent to which people with learning disabilities are enjoying greater social inclusion than previously. This is a difficult question to answer and is complicated by the fact that there is no single definition of social inclusion or exclusion. As a result, thoughts about the most effective ways to promote social inclusion vary. According to the Scottish Executive website (www.scotland.gov.uk), social inclusion can be defined as being about:

> reducing inequalities between the least advantaged groups and communities and the rest of society by closing the opportunity gap and ensuring that support reaches those who need it most. (Scottish Executive, n.d.)

In 2004, the Scottish Executive introduced six Closing the Opportunity Gap targets, which focused on individuals, neighbourhoods and communities as well as the structural barriers that can be regarded as contributing to social exclusion. The targets focused on barriers in relation to health, employment and communities. They recommended increasing the chances of sustained employment for vulnerable or disadvantaged groups by increasing confidence and skills. In doing so, it was argued, the likelihood of financial exclusion was reduced. As well as a focus on improving employability of disadvantaged individuals, disadvantaged neighbourhoods were also to be regenerated in order that people living there could benefit from improved quality of life, improved health status and improved access to high quality services (Scottish Executive, 2004b). These are issues that will be explored in greater detail throughout the course of this book.

Levitas (2004) provides a helpful account of the different ways in which social exclusion and inclusion can be viewed. She outlines three different discourses of social exclusion. Of particular relevance in present-day Britain is the social integrationist discourse, which focuses on paid employment as the route out of social exclusion. This can be problematic as it downplays the problems of in-work poverty, low wages, poor conditions and insecurity. The redistributive discourse, however, is more helpful, focusing as it does on extending citizenship rights, reducing inequality and redistribution of wealth as the route out of social exclusion. This would suggest that value should be placed on the differing roles people play in society rather than focusing solely on paid employment. This would suggest, for example, that spending time in a day centre with friends and peers should be valued equally alongside paid employment.

The social model of disability

It would appear that the development of many policies in relation to people with learning disabilities in the UK in recent years has been influenced by the social model of disability. Broadly speaking, in many spheres there is a growing rhetoric of commitment to the social model of disability and this is echoed in policies of inclusion for people with disabilities in areas such as education. It should be kept in mind, however, that elements of the medical model of disability still influence certain policies to some extent. *The Same As You*? (Scottish Executive, 2000a), is clearly influenced by the social model of disability as well as by principles of normalisation. The development of the social model of disability alongside the growth of the disability movement since the 1970s has been well documented in the literature by academics and disability activists alike (for example, Finkelstein, 1981; Oliver, 1990, 1996; Morris, 1991; Barnes *et al.*, 1996, 1999; and Shakespeare, 1998). It is important to highlight the impact that the disability movement in general and the social model of disability in particular have had in terms of changing the way in which disabled people are viewed and treated in society.

Prior to the 1970s a medical or individual model of disability dominated (and arguably still does in some spheres). This model traces its roots back to the late 19th century and is based on the premise that disability stems from impairment or illness and is the result of personal tragedy. Attention is focused on the individual and the ways in which he or she can be treated or rehabilitated to fit into society. Medical and rehabilitation professionals have a key role to play in this process and it has been argued that it is in the interests of these groups of professionals to maintain the view of disability as personal tragedy in order to validate their own role in society (see, for example, Oliver, 1996). This notion of a medical or individual model of disability can be seen clearly to influence social and public policy over the last two centuries. The eugenics movement of the early 20th century that argued for the sterilisation of 'mentally defected' or 'mentally retarded' adult women can be seen as a classic example of a movement that was influenced by a medical model of disability. Examples of legislation at that time that were influenced by the medical model of disability include the Mental Deficiency Act of 1913, which made provision for the detention in long-stay hospitals of women with mental deficiencies who bore illegitimate children. It can perhaps be seen as testimony to the disability movement and the social model of disability that such practices can now seem shocking, yet the abortion of an impaired foetus is still seen in many quarters as an acceptable practice (see Swain and French, 2000, for an interesting discussion around whether it is 'better to die than be disabled').

The policies of segregation and institutionalisation for people with a range of disabilities that prevailed for much of the last century were also influenced by a medical model of disability. As discussed above, until relatively recently it was common practice for people with disabilities to live outside their communities in long-stay hospitals (Stalker and Hunter, 1999). The government move to close these hospitals (see, for example, Whoriskey, 2003) can be viewed as a largely positive development (although there are complex arguments around the pros and cons of this – see Cattermole *et al.*, 1990; Stalker and Hunter, 1999; Forrester-Jones *et al.*, 2002 for a more detailed discussion) and one that was influenced by the social model of disability. Likewise the move towards mainstream education for young people with a range of disabilities has meant that it is no longer acceptable to segregate young people in special settings, unless there is a 'good reason' (i.e. the education of that child or other children will suffer) (Department for Education and Skills, 2001). It can be argued therefore that the social model of disability has been prominent in terms of influencing policy and has had an impact upon the ways in which people with disabilities are viewed by society as a whole. Albrecht (quoted in Hales, 1996, p. 67) sums this up well: 'the social meanings given to impairment and disability shape public and institutional responses to these conditions ....'

However, the process has been more complex than a simple move from a medical model to a social model of disability, and elements of the medical model are still significant in today's society. Welfare to work policies, for example, impose a simple binary distinction between being able to work and not able to work. This has resulted in an inflexibility that has created barriers for disabled people who wish to move into the labour market. Likewise, the social model of disability has not been without its critics, particularly among 'second-wave' disability writers who argue that, conceptually, the social model may not be a useful tool to assist in understanding the experiences of all groups of disabled people. Some writers, for example, argue that the social model of disability does not adequately represent their experiences as a result of not taking their impairment into account. The majority of disability writers, academics and activists would stand by most of the principles of the social model of disability, while arguing for a reworking of the social model that incorporates personal experience, difference and impairment. Shakespeare and Watson (1997) draw on feminist and post-modern accounts to point out that recognition of difference within the disability community is 'long overdue'. It is beyond the scope of this book to discuss the complex debates around the usefulness or otherwise of the social model of disability. What is of note here is its undoubted influence on policies relating to people with learning disabilities in Scotland and the rest of the UK.

Theories of citizenship

One of the key aims of this chapter has been to show the ways in which expectations around people with learning disabilities have changed in recent years. People with learning disabilities have become increasingly present within their local communities. This community presence, however, does not always readily translate into participation within these communities. Despite the difficulties in participation which will be outlined in the remainder of the book, people with learning disabilities can increasingly expect to take part in the worlds of education, employment and leisure and increasingly expect to be treated as equal citizens. Disability writers such as Oliver (1996) have used arguments around citizenship to argue for equal rights for disabled people. However, the link between citizenship rights and obligations has continued to emphasise paid employment as a key duty or obligation in order to gain entitlement to certain benefits or rights. The promotion of social inclusion by the elevation of obligation remains an important element of New Labour's thinking in the 'third way' (Lund, 1999). Examples include the duty of those on Jobseeker's Allowance to actively seek paid employment and the allocation of a personal adviser to all new benefit claimants. New Labour has continued to argue that paid work is the way out of poverty or social exclusion.

All of this raises questions about the position of disabled people in relation to rights, entitlements and citizenship. Lund (1999) has drawn on the work of Marshall (1981), who argued that the services offered to disabled people were inspired by compassion rather than interest. As a result, the rights of disabled people are moral rights born from compassion. These rights, it is argued, are weaker than those rights attached to obligations. As a result disabled people can only claim full citizenship rights if these rights are attached to corresponding obligations such as a duty to participate in paid employment (see also Hyde, 2000). To make matters even more difficult, Stepney *et al.* (1999) highlight the point that central to New Labour's programme on poverty is the idea that equality must be based on equality of opportunity rather than equality of outcome, thus putting disabled people and other marginalised groups at a disadvantage (as disabled people would be likely to require additional support to achieve equality of outcome). Indeed, the identical treatment of disabled people may actually serve to perpetuate the effects of past discrimination if additional action is not taken (Northway, 1997). The links between rights and obligations are apparent in New Labour's welfare reforms in relation to disabled people. Social security has been gradually tightened and new work-related programmes have been introduced (Drake, 2000). The government has restructured social security so the system focuses more narrowly on people with very severe impairments, older disabled people and disabled children. For disabled people of working age, the system has become increasingly oriented towards entry into the workforce (Drake, 2000).

Walmsley (1991) has argued that 'citizenship, as it has traditionally been conceived, has seemed an impossible status for people with learning disabilities'. The emphasis on rights and obligations, while initially promising, serves to further exclude disabled people as a result of the continued focus on paid employment, not only as the way out of poverty but as the key to other rights and services. A focus on supply side measures that are intended to deal with individuals rather than attempting to deal with disabling employment practices mean that those disabled people unable to work have to rely on moral rights born from compassion. As the literature points out, these rights appear to be weaker and so disabled individuals may not have access to the full rights of citizenship.

A more helpful perspective for people with learning disabilities may involve drawing upon feminist concepts of citizenship and care. Feminist writers have argued that the concept of citizenship, with its focus on waged labour as the key to rights and entitlements, has been oppressive to women. Svenhuijsen (2000) has drawn on the work of Giddens (1998) and has argued that he repeats an outdated division between the category of 'self-sufficient workers' and 'dependent others' based on the independent male worker as the paradigm for citizenship (Svenhuijsen, 2000, p. 19). However, Harris (2002) has pointed to the ways in which caring is a socially constructed concept, with the position of the carer varying with changes in welfare regime. As mentioned earlier, the strategy adopted by New Labour has been to focus on social inclusion through paid employment. As a result, unpaid work has been de-valued, although Harris (2002) has argued that the work done by carers is an exception to this rule as caring is represented as a valued activity and an expression of citizenship obligation. Not all writers would agree with Harris's position that caring is a valued activity. Indeed, others such as Svenhuijsen (2000) would argue that caring as an activity is not valued highly enough. Again using the work of Giddens (1998) as an example, she argues that he fails to address the importance of caring in society.

The emphasis on caring as a citizenship obligation has led to tension between carers and those being cared for (see Walmsley, 1991; Harris, 2002; Watson *et al.*, 2004). Harris has argued that it has led to:

> a situation whereby carers' voices are privileged over the voices of cared-for people with the former being portrayed as virtuously active and the latter seen as a drain on resources. (Harris, 2002, p. 277)

Watson *et al.* (2004) point out that over-simplistic binaries such as 'carers' and 'dependent people' obscure the reciprocity in human relationships and the 'unpredictability, mutability and often multiple subjectivities of all our lives' (p. 344). Williams (2001) puts it well when she points out that at different times and in different places and in different ways we will all need to be cared for.

The dominant model of citizenship is based solely on active participation, usefulness and self-reliance from which many recipients of care or other disabled people will feel excluded (Harris, 2002). A more inclusive approach or model takes into account the different roles played by different people within society and values each of these roles. It is increasingly recognised that binary concepts of independence and dependence or 'carer' and 'dependent person' (Watson *et al.*, 2004) are overly simplistic and do not offer a helpful way of understanding the experiences of women or other groups in society. Feminists and disability writers have pointed to the concept of interdependence as a more useful way to understand the experiences of women and disabled people. A feminist ethic of care (see, for example, Orme, 2002) would argue that individuals can only exist because they are members of various networks of care and responsibility:

> a democratic ethic of care starts off from the idea that everyone needs care and is capable of care giving and that a democratic society should enable its members to give both these activities a meaningful place in their lives if they want. (Svenhuijsen, 2000, p. 16)

In line with feminist arguments, then, disability writers would argue for renewed concepts of independence and interdependence. For disabled people, independence is not about self-care activities such as being able to cook and wash for oneself. It is about being in control of and making decisions about one's life (Morris, 1991; Reindal, 1999). Reindal (1999) argues that if the human condition is viewed as one of interdependency and vulnerability this leads to an understanding of independence as partnership. Independence therefore becomes a two-way responsibility and not solely an individual ability.

Recent policy developments in the field of learning disability have been influenced by both the social model of disability and the concept of citizenship. It is beyond the scope of this book to look in depth at the complex debate around the helpfulness or otherwise of both of these concepts. What is important for the reader to bear in mind, however, is the ways in which policy developments and service provision have shifted from overly medicalised perspectives where the individual should be segregated and 'treated' to more social perspectives which look at the role which society plays in creating disabling barriers. Policies influenced by the social model suggest that the individual has a right to be included and to participate within mainstream society. This shift has by no means been straightforward. This book does not suggest that medical perspectives are no longer influential. Nor indeed does it suggest that concepts such as the social model of disability or certain concepts of citizenship cannot in some contexts be oppressive to people with learning disabilities. The shift in attitudes and perspective, however, is significant and the concepts of citizenship, the social model of disability and social inclusion will be discussed throughout the rest of the book. The following chapters will look in more detail at four key areas in the lives of people with learning disabilities – education and further education, training and employment, health and social work.

CHAPTER 2

Moving On from School

This chapter will look in some detail at the ways in which young people with learning disabilities are prepared for the transition to adulthood. The chapter will set out the range of options that are likely to be available to young people upon leaving school and will critically assess the likely impact of recent changes in policy. In particular, the chapter will explore the potential impact of:

- the Introduction of the Education (Additional Support for Learning) (Scotland) Act 2005;
- the recommendations of the Beattie Committee, published in the report *Implementing Inclusiveness, Realising Potential* (Scottish Executive, 1999a);
- changes to the ways in which young people receive careers guidance from Careers Scotland and (the Connexions service in England and Wales).

Education: A move towards greater inclusion?

The transition process starts while young people are still at school. Until very recently, procedures for preparing for this transition were governed by the Education (Scotland) Act 1980. This Act placed a duty on education authorities to provide adequate and efficient school education for their area, including for children with special educational needs (SEN). Authorities had a duty placed on them to find out which children in their area had special educational needs that needed to be reviewed. They had to open and keep a record of needs for any child who following an assessment was deemed to have SEN. The Act also placed a duty on authorities to provide a Future Needs Assessment (FNA) for any child with SEN who they felt might benefit from local authority services after leaving school. Children attending both mainstream and special schools were entitled to be assessed for a record of needs.

In recent years there has been a move towards a much more inclusive education policy throughout the UK (Riddell *et al.*, 2000; 2002b). In England and Wales, one of the key features of the 1996 Education Act was the clear expectation that pupils with a Statement of Special Educational Needs (a similar document to the record of needs) would be educated in mainstream schools. However, a parent's wish for their child to be educated in a mainstream setting could still be refused in a small minority of cases where 'the child's inclusion would be incompatible with the efficient education of other children' (Department for Education and Skills, 2001, p. 35). In Scotland, the Executive wished to see a larger number of children educated in mainstream schools, while still recognising the importance of special units and schools for a small number of children with more complex or profound needs (Riddell and Banks, 2001). The Standards in Scotland's Schools etc. Act 2000 required all children to be educated in mainstream schools unless it would not be suited to the ability of the child; it would be inappropriate for the provision of effective education to other children with whom the child would be educated; or it would result in unreasonable public expenditure being incurred. Although these developments may be viewed as a step forward in terms of inclusion some might argue that they do not go far enough. In Scotland, for example, the Executive is not specific in terms of the number of children they wish to see educated in mainstream schools, making progress difficult to measure. In addition, clauses about the effective education of other children could perhaps be used by some education authorities or departments as a 'get-out clause'.

The Education (Additional Support for Learning) (Scotland) Act 2004

The move towards greater inclusion within mainstream education has been accompanied by a redefinition of the group of young people classed as having SEN. The Education (Additional Support for Learning) (Scotland) Act (the ASN Act), which was passed in 2004 and came into force on 14 November 2005, emphasised inclusion as one of its key principles. It resulted in the replacement of the category SEN with a new category of 'additional support needs' (ASN). This category covers a much broader group of children and young people. As well as children and young people with a range of disabilities, the ASN category includes children with emotional, social and behavioural (ESB) problems, asylum seeker and refugee children, traveller children and children leaving local authority care. This arguably better reflects the changing make-up of modern society but this is a potentially large group of children and young people, many of whom may require intensive support at various times during their educational career and beyond. The resource implications therefore are likely to be significant. The Scottish Executive, in the explanatory document that accompanied the bill, *Moving Forward! Additional Support for Learning*, explained its vision as wishing:

> to see an education system that is inclusive, welcomes diversity and provides an equal opportunity for all our children to develop

> their personality, skills and abilities to their fullest potential. (Scottish Executive, 2003b, Introduction)

The bill arose due to concerns that existing assessment and recording systems for children with SEN were outdated and overly bureaucratic. The 2004 Act introduced a number of new measures such as the abolition of the record of needs. The record of needs was replaced by a co-ordinated support plan, but only children and young people who are likely to need services from agencies other than the education department will be eligible for one of these. Education authorities still have a duty to identify those children with additional support needs and address these needs (Scottish Executive, 2005b). However:

> they [education authorities] will not have to formally assess every child to establish whether they have any additional support needs but they will be expected to take steps to ensure that the reasons for a child's lack of progress are identified and appropriate action is taken. (Scottish Executive, 2003c)

In addition to these measures, the right of appeal for parents was strengthened through a new system of mediation, appeals and tribunals. Alongside this, however, was a greater emphasis on parents' roles and responsibilities in their child's education, thus emphasising the commitment of New Labour to linking rights with obligations. Riddell (2004) has identified some areas of concern with this new legislation. In particular there may be new difficulties in ensuring that a child with ASN is correctly identified, given that education authorities are no longer expected to formally assess children in all cases. Furthermore it is no longer necessary to have a multi-professional assessment of a child's needs and this may lead to incorrect diagnosis (Riddell, 2004). She points to research on the Individual Education Plans (IEPs) which shows that in the majority of cases health and social work professionals were not involved in the assessments (see also Millward *et al.*, 2002; Kane *et al.*, 2003 for a more detailed discussion). Since co-ordinated support plans take on many of the features of IEPs it is likely that multi-professional involvement will decrease. Riddell (2004) argues that there is a danger that the nature of assessment conducted and the nature of the professionals involved will predetermine the nature of the needs identified.

There is also a danger that shifting responsibility onto parents and strengthening their rights of appeal may lead to greater inequalities among young people. Riddell (2004) refers to research on the SEN trials in England, established under the 1993 Education Act, that suggests that rates of appeal are higher in the London boroughs, the South East and parts of the North West than other parts of the country. Parents from minority ethnic groups are particularly unlikely to appeal (Riddell, 2004). It would seem therefore that the ASN Act, which has been designed to result in greater inclusion and equality for children and young people, may actually result in confusion and inequality. Widening the category of young people with ASN may result in greater numbers of children competing for scarce resources, as the following quote from the author's own research[1] suggests:

> you know [names primary school] they gave me an example of one of their classes round about primary four where all but four kids would have additional support needs because they identified dyslexia at an early time, because they had EAL pupils, English Additional Language, because they had a few ADHDs [attention deficit hyperactivity disorder], they had somebody who was visually impaired and it built up. (Representative, local authority education department)

At the same time confusion arises because not all children with disabilities will have a co-ordinated support plan and not all children with a co-ordinated support plan will be disabled. This may lead to inequalities that will be exacerbated by whether or not parents decide to appeal against decisions made by the education authority. The growing amount of administration and bureaucracy created by the existence of various education plans for different children might best be addressed by offering an assessment and education plan to all children who want one regardless of disability.

Options available for young people with learning disabilities upon leaving school

Young people with learning disabilities have a greater range of options available to them than ever before upon leaving school. Traditionally, young people with learning disabilities would have been expected to move on from school to an adult resource centre or day centre. Much research has been highly critical of the role of day centres in the lives of young people. Barnes (1990), for example, argued that although day centres were regarded by many policy makers and practitioners as training centres, in

1 The author's own research, undertaken as part of her doctoral thesis, explored the transition from childhood to adulthood for young people with learning disabilities. The research had a particular focus on further education, training and employment opportunities for young people upon leaving school. The research adopted a case study approach and involved working in depth with twenty young people and the 'significant others' in their lives, including parents, social workers, lecturers, careers advisers and employers. Where quoted, interviewees' names have been changed to preserve anonymity.

actual fact they acted as 'holding centres' which did not accomplish their aim of preparing people for open or sheltered employment. Research by Riddell *et al.* (2001) would appear to support these findings. Participants in their research valued contact with their friends at the day centre. However, they found the activities that they did there neither interesting nor stimulating. In addition, research has shown that the day centre is not always the most cost-effective option. A day centre place costs around £7,000 a year, compared with £3,200 for a Training for Work placement (funded by Scottish Enterprise) and £4,760 for a Work Step place (funded by the Department of Work and Pensions and run by Jobcentre Plus (Scottish Executive, 2000a). A range of initiatives have meant that disabled people, their families, policy makers and practitioners expect more than life in an adult training centre. These include the reconfiguration of local authority day services (see Glasgow City Council, 2000 for a discussion of this at a local level) and the introduction of a range of measures to encourage disabled people into the labour market, such as the New Deal for Disabled People. Figures from the Scottish Executive (2007a) suggest that by 2006, around 27% of adults with a learning disability known to local authorities in Scotland benefited from some form of alternative day activity (as opposed to the traditional adult training centre or day centre placement).

The figures outlined in Chapter 1 show clearly that the majority of young people with learning disabilities go on to some form of further education upon leaving school. According to Mitchell (1999), post-school training has become a significant part of many disabled young people's lives, partly due to the expansion of further education as discussed in Chapter 1 (see also Riddell *et al.*, 2001). This is supported by figures from Glasgow City Council (2001) which illustrate that 50% of young people leaving special school in Glasgow in 2000 moved on to further education after leaving school. In Scotland as a whole in 2000/01, 19% of school leavers moved on to further education. By 2005/06, this figure had increased to 23% (Scottish Executive, 2007a). Figures were not broken down by additional support need.

According to Mitchell (1999), further education college provided an opportunity for those young people who had previously attended a special school to move on to a more adult, mainstream environment. This is supported by the experiences of the young people who participated in the author's own research:

> it was just meeting new people and knowing that I could call lecturers by their first name like you couldn't at school. (Joanne, 18)

> I was thinking about that [getting a job straight from school] but then I got scared. But now I've got the experience [gained at

> college] to go to work. If they offered me a full-time job now I'd probably take it. (Craig, 21)

Despite the promise of a more mainstream setting, in reality young people's experiences of college continued to be separately organised and managed. Often, there was little interaction with non-disabled peers, and work experience (a key feature of many college courses) was not open to everyone (Mitchell, 1999). Wider socio-economic factors such as the availability of work placements and the support offered by employers were important excluding mechanisms. In addition, the opportunity structure was frequently mediated and interpreted by professional assessments and judgements of what was feasible. This is supported by the author's own findings:

> He [the teacher] said I should go to college and do the Step course 'cos it would give me more confidence and 'cos I'm usually shy to people and he said it would give me more confidence to talk more to people and give me more qualifications. (Natalie, 18)

> and you don't want to set somebody up not to succeed, you know, so you look for alternatives that would have been possible and would have moved [name of person] forward. (Career advisor)

These findings are supported by other research in this area. Riddell *et al.* (2001), in their study *The Learning Society and People with Learning Disabilities*, found that in two of the fieldwork areas studied few choices were available to young people with learning difficulties. They were allocated college places rather than choosing from different options. Indeed, they argued that the local enterprise companies and further education providers were informed by a utilitarian model of social justice which resulted in the marginalisation of young people with learning difficulties.

The increasing marketisation of further education has targeted additional resources on those with special needs (see Chapter 1), but this has not balanced out disadvantages suffered by people with disabilities in the labour market. If anything, the targeting of young people with learning disabilities further disadvantages them by labelling them as 'special' and removing them from the mainstream. Premium funding provided for the education of students with additional support needs has in some cases led to an increase in segregated provision (Watson and Farmakopoulou, 2003). Indeed, Riddell and colleagues (2005) have pointed out that further education colleges were less inclusive than mainstream schools where disabled students would be expected to spend at least part of their day with their peers. In addition, the absence of supported and open employment opportunities for young people with learning difficulties meant the most likely destination after college was an adult training centre, despite the policy rhetoric and changing expectations outlined above.

Similarly, Watson and Farmakopoulou (2003) found that, despite the attempts of government policies for inclusive learning in Scotland and across the UK as a whole, the majority of provision for disabled students in colleges remained segregated. In addition, certain groups of students appeared to have been in the same class over several years or appeared to move from one segregated course to another within the same or different colleges. Such courses did not always lead to qualifications and the main benefits of college appeared to be social. Indeed, research by Pitt and Curtin (2004) found that for disabled students attending a specialist further education college, far from feeling socially segregated, it appeared that there were positive personal and social affects of being with similarly disabled people (these young people had previously reported experiences of bullying while attending mainstream school).

The research suggests therefore that the primary benefit of further education for disabled young people appears to be social and Watson and Farmakopoulou (2003) suggest that the emphasis of further education should perhaps shift from human to social capital principles such as citizenship, capacity building and empowerment. The difficulties for young disabled people in terms of gaining marketable skills relating to qualifications and employability within a mainstream further education setting have been highlighted. Yet, despite these difficulties, young disabled people continue to aspire to employment (as do disadvantaged young people within the general population) (see Mitchell, 1999; Smyth and McConkey, 2003; Burchardt, 2005 for a discussion of disabled young people's aspirations in relation to paid employment, and Johnston *et al.*, 2000 for a more detailed discussion of the aspirations of disadvantaged young people in the general population) and, overall, have an optimistic and pragmatic view of the future (see Conners and Stalker, 2002). Recent research on the transitional experiences of young disabled people suggests that the transition to paid employment continues to be problematic. This will be discussed in greater detail in the following chapter.

Post-sixteen education, training and employment policy: the Beattie Report

Given the difficulties identified in terms of making the transition from school to further education, training and employment, the Beattie Committee was established to take forward the government's commitment to increasing the participation and attainment of young people set out in the White Paper *Opportunity Scotland* (Scottish Executive, 1998). Although not targeted directly at young people with learning disabilities, the committee focused on those young people who needed additional support to participate and live up to their potential in the post-school period. A particular focus of attention was young people who were disadvantaged or disaffected and 'in danger of slipping out of society' (Scottish Executive, 1999a). This included young people with learning disabilities as well as young people with physical disabilities, mental health problems, low educational attainment, poor basic skills and social, emotional and behavioural difficulties. Again this can be seen as widening the group to be covered by the legislation from the traditional notions and definitions of disability and special educational needs.

The key recommendation of the report was that the principle of inclusiveness should underpin all post-school guidance, education and training. Key issues identified were the transitions from school to college or training and ultimately to employment; the assessment and identification of education and training needs; staff development and training; adequacy and appropriateness of provision; arrangements for transition and progression; and involving employers. The committee made around 80 recommendations, all based around the core principle of inclusiveness. It suggested that all young people on leaving school should have access to adequate and appropriate learning provision within a learning environment matching their needs, abilities and wishes (Scottish Executive, 1999a, para. 2.1).

The recommendations led to the establishment of 17 inclusiveness projects across the country. The Scottish Executive Enterprise and Lifelong Learning Department allocated £15 million in April 2001 to establish the projects, which led to key worker teams being set up across the country. Key workers were appointed to each area to offer support to young people. They were thought to offer a single point of contact and would guide and support the young person. Part of their role was to act on the young person's behalf in negotiating and agreeing the most appropriate packages of provision (Scottish Executive, 1999a). The main focus of the key worker was on employability and their role was to be complemented by that of the mentor, who would offer support on a more informal basis to the young person and their family or carer. Interestingly, the report stated that key workers would be appointed in each area to offer support to young people who 'needed it' (Scottish Executive, 1999a). However, demand far outweighed supply and most areas have had to establish eligibility criteria for the service, such as being a young care leaver. This may raise questions as to how inclusive the service actually is.

The report identified the provision of guidance and support at times of transition as being of critical importance. Evidence from focus groups carried out on behalf of the Beattie Committee suggested that guidance and support can often come too late. As a result, it was recommended that preparation for transition should occur as soon as possible. In addition the committee recognised that ongoing support for young people at times of transition was essential and recommended that colleges and training providers in collaboration with Careers Scotland and other agencies should identify ways in which ongoing support and guidance could be enhanced (Scottish Executive, 1999a).

To this end, several relevant developments occurred. These included Get Ready for Work, a new training programme for 16- and 17-year-olds with additional support needs which replaced the Special Needs Skillseekers Programme. (Training opportunities for people with learning disabilities will be discussed in more detail in the next chapter.) Another development was the introduction of the BRITE initiative, which offers national training opportunities to all colleges in Scotland, distributes and supports assistive technology work stations for each college in Scotland, and provides a virtual staffroom for all further education staff (see www.brite.ac.uk). This initiative was designed to improve staff skills, create equal access across the sector for clients and support inclusion. In addition, funding was made available to contribute towards the development of a Post-School Psychological Service (PSPS). Sixteen pathfinder projects were set up across local authority areas in Scotland and between 2004 and 2006 they were to demonstrate service delivery at local, cluster and strategic level. Consultation by the national development officers (Boyle *et al.*, 2003) highlighted support from key stakeholders for a post-school psychological service. Resource limitations, however, meant that the input was likely to be at a strategic level rather than casework with individual young people.

As yet, little research has been conducted into the progress being made in implementing the recommendations of the Beattie Committee or to look at the effectiveness of the developments outlined above. However, progress has been monitored by a National Action Group and independent evaluations have been commissioned (see Adams and Smart, 2005; Scottish Executive, 2005c; Scottish Executive, 2005d). The progress report of the National Action Group (Scottish Executive, 2003e) suggested that:

> a great deal has already been achieved .... However, there are still far too many young people who slip through the net. And this is clearly a challenge that we continue to face. (Scottish Executive, 2003e)

The report highlighted what it termed a 'number of highly positive developments' such as the BRITE initiative outlined above. It recognised that some developments such as transitions to employment and mentoring were still in their very early stages and that more needed to be done to improve certain areas such as the monitoring of the impact of the developments in terms of tracking the activities and outcomes for the young people. To this extent, Careers Scotland has developed a performance management system in an attempt to generate information about hard and soft outcomes (Scottish Executive, 2003e). However, as Riddell and colleagues (2005) note, this information has not always been collected in a consistent and coherent way. It has been particularly difficult to measure progress on soft outcomes such as increasing self-confidence. Work continues to improve ways of measuring outcomes.

The report also highlighted seven priority areas for further development. These included the continued development of key worker support for vulnerable young people. Another priority identified by the report was the need to ensure appropriate training provision. In particular a need was identified for an improved quality assurance framework and key performance indicators for hard outcomes such as employment and softer indicators of client progression such as increased self-confidence or motivation. Improving transitions to employment was also identified as a priority. To this end supported employment projects became operational in seven of the inclusiveness projects in April 2003. Supported employment developments were at an earlier stage than most of the developments stemming from the Beattie recommendations as a result of greater than anticipated difficulties in starting up the projects, and in particular finding supported employment placements for the young people involved.

Independent evaluations of the inclusiveness projects and the supported employment projects were commissioned in 2003. The national evaluation of the inclusiveness projects reported a largely successful picture, although projects had under-estimated the scale of the task and had not achieved all that they had intended within the time given (Scottish Executive, 2003d). The figures available showed that inclusiveness clients had made 7,611 entries into employment, training and educational placements during the first two years of operation. However, these figures must be treated with some caution as the data is based upon client interventions which could be multiple in the case of a single client. Also, Riddell and colleagues (2005) point out that it is not clear whether these outcomes can only be attributed to the success of the projects, as no baseline data is currently available. In addition, the data has suggested that sustained entries of more than three months into employment, training and educational placements have been achieved in 6,550 instances. This suggests that the inclusiveness projects are succeeding in achieving a high proportion of sustainable outcomes – 86% of all entries – for their clients (Scottish Executive, 2003d). Given the well-documented difficulties that this client group have experienced in the past in terms of sustaining placements (see, for example, Hirst and Baldwin, 1994; Hendey and Pascall, 2002; Morris, 2002; Stalker, 2002), this would appear to be a significant achievement.

Overall, the report suggested that the inclusiveness projects have added value by developing local partnership networks aimed at improving service provision for young people who would otherwise have been at significant risk of 'falling through gaps' in the existing service infrastructure. They have also assisted in the development of tools, systems and products designed to assist young people making the transition from school or care and they have provided a sharper focus on employability within existing services (Scottish Executive, 2003c). The key worker approach has been particularly valued by clients, with over 70% of clients rejecting the statement that their key worker was 'just another worker they had to see'. The report suggests that this may have been due to the flexibility and intensity of support offered by key workers. Three quarters of clients had seen their key worker at least once a fortnight and over 40% had seen them more often than this. Over 70% of clients were very satisfied with the support received from the key worker (Scottish Executive, 2003c, p. iii).

The final report, published by the Scottish Executive in 2005 (Scottish Executive, 2005c) painted a similar picture to that outlined in the interim report described here, although the figures that suggest that the service helps clients achieve and sustain hard targets such as paid employment are qualified somewhat. Overall, clients have shown considerable progress in terms of soft skills such as increased self-confidence (in 88% of cases) and possess greater employability (because of improvements in, for instance, self-esteem, leadership, time-management, motivation and emotional control). Despite this, hard targets or positive outcomes continued to elude many of the clients. Although the proportion of clients in employment increased from 15% to 20%, the number becoming unemployed also increased, from 18% to 35% over the same period (Scottish Executive, 2005c).

The developments stemming from the recommendations of the Beattie Committee have clearly had some success in terms of introducing more inclusive services to assist young people who are in danger of 'slipping through the net' to make the transition from school to further education, training and employment. There is, however, still room for considerable improvement. Scotland has a higher proportion of 16–19-year-olds not in employment, education or training (NEET). Scotland also has a higher unemployment rate among 16–24-year-olds than the rest of the UK (13.6% and 10.5% respectively) and is ranked 21 in a sample of 31 OECD countries (Scottish Executive, 2003e). It would appear therefore that, although things may be moving in the right direction, more needs to be done to assist young people into further education, training and employment. To this end the Scottish Executive launched six Closing the Opportunity Gap objectives in July 2004, in order to increase the chances of sustained employment for vulnerable and disadvantaged groups, to improve the confidence and skills of the most disadvantaged children and young people, and to reduce the vulnerability of low income families to financial exclusion and multiple debts (Scottish Executive, 2004b) As mentioned above, this creates dilemmas as to which group of young people should be the focus of policy intervention. One thing that does remain clear, however, is the very definite focus on employability by the various projects and service interventions. This reflects New Labour's overall goal of encouraging as many people as possible into employment.

Discussion

The overall climate in education in Scotland is currently one of inclusion. Policy drivers have promoted lifelong learning as an attainable goal for everyone, regardless of age, gender, ethnicity or disability. Education can be regarded as a route out of poverty and social exclusion, enabling people to build human and social capital and contribute to society as active citizens. For people with learning disabilities, however, caution is advised when interpreting what can at first glance be regarded as largely positive developments. As a result of the Education (Additional Support for Learning) Act 2004, the group of young people who are targeted for intervention has changed. The effect of the Act, discussed above, will be to widely extend the group of young people who traditionally receive support. The key feature would appear to be a move away from a more targeted provision of services to a much more inclusive model that recognises the needs of a greater number of young people. While greater recognition of need should be welcomed, widening the net in this manner may result in those with less need getting a greater share of services. It may be that in order to access certain services having a learning disability is no longer enough, unless it is accompanied by a range of additional support needs. Young people with learning disabilities increasingly have to compete with a much larger group for resources and it is possible that this will affect the services they receive. There is some evidence from the interviews with Beattie key workers and the inclusiveness projects that suggests that young people with learning disabilities cannot always be a priority for key worker support:

> That has caused some I don't know about difficulties but tensions within the strategy group that oversee our project because the people from the various councils who represent, that are supportive of the strategy, it includes two principal psychologists, two principal educational psychologists and a special needs co-ordinator from the third council, so all steeped in the record of needs, special school or integrated in mainstream but record of needs type child ... And that was who Beattie was originally focusing on and that's who they saw as who this was about but other reps from the

> strategy group come from economic planning within the councils and from, em, the SIP [Social Inclusion Partnership] partnership type backgrounds, social inclusion partnership and of course their take on it is rather different. They see this as being about issues to do with disadvantage, economic exclusion, chaotic lifestyles and sometimes at some of the meetings you can see that neither side understands where the other side's coming from in the, you know, its just interesting I think. (Inclusiveness project co-ordinator)

Scotland has tended to lag behind other European countries in terms of the qualifications attained by young people upon leaving school and also the number of young people moving on to further education, training and employment (see Scottish Executive, 2003a for a discussion of progress towards social justice targets). As a result, the focus of the Beattie Implementation Team at the Scottish Executive has increasingly moved to young care leavers, who have particularly poor outcomes in relation to education, employment and training, and the NEET group (see Howison, 2003; Raffe, 2003; Scottish Executive, 2005f for a more detailed discussion). It should be noted, however, that many young people with learning disabilities may not be in education, employment and training. The result is that they are likely to be part of the NEET group by default.

Although the education of children and adults with learning disabilities is increasingly taking place in mainstream settings, this chapter has shown that this does not necessarily result in greater social inclusion. Young people who have been classified as having a learning disability are less likely to leave school with qualifications. The majority are likely to go on to further education where they will be channelled onto a special needs course, regardless of whether they attended a mainstream school. Within the further education college, young people with learning disabilities are unlikely to mix with their non-disabled peers and again are less likely to attain qualifications. The most likely outcome for young people with learning disabilities upon completion of their course is to undertake another course (the revolving door syndrome) or to take-up a placement on a training or employment programme. The next chapter reviews the support services and training and employment programmes available for young people and adults with learning disabilities.

CHAPTER 3

Finding and Sustaining Training and Employment

A key focus of the review of learning disability services in Scotland was to improve employment opportunities for people with learning disabilities. This chapter will outline the current situation for people with learning disabilities in relation to training and employment. It will discuss some of the barriers faced by this group in terms of attaining and sustaining a placement and will provide an overview of policy direction and service provision in this area, the aim of which is to support people into the labour market.

People with learning disabilities and other disabilities continue to face a range of barriers when it comes to accessing and sustaining training or paid employment. These barriers include inadequate and inflexible support services which do not meet the needs of people with disabilities, and the benefits system. These barriers and the attempts to overcome them through a range of policy and service initiatives are the focus of this chapter. Morris (2002) suggested that the variability of support services to assist disabled people into employment, such as supported employment projects, is a significant factor. The availability of such projects varies locally and many projects are short term and insecure. In addition, specialist schools and colleges appear to lack information about such opportunities, for they rarely refer young disabled people to supported employment agencies (Morris, 2002), the end result being that young disabled people are 'hurtling into a void' upon leaving school (Morris, 1999). Often the attitudes and low expectations of disabled people, their families and various practitioners result in employment not being considered as a serious option, particularly for those with more significant impairments. A similar picture emerged for young disabled people making the transition from childhood to adulthood in Scotland (Stalker, 2002). The benefits system was identified as a significant barrier which can often deter disabled people from looking for work. This is particularly the case when the person's benefits make up a substantial proportion of the household income (Weston, 2002).

These findings are supported by the work of Pascall and Hendey (2002), who examined the transitional experiences of young people with a range of disabilities in relation to both paid employment and independent living. They identified a range of barriers to paid employment for people with disabilities including a lack of qualifications, employer attitudes and the benefits system. They also pointed out that young people with disabilities found it extremely difficult to achieve both paid employment and independent living. The benefits system had a crucial role to play and respondents in their study felt that the benefits system was often at the heart of their difficulties in combining different aspects of adult status. The type of work available meant that young people were unlikely to earn enough to pay for accommodation and personal assistance costs, making benefits a more attractive option.

Get Ready for Work training programme

In terms of training programmes, younger people with learning disabilities in Scotland are most likely to access the Get Ready for Work training programme upon leaving school or further education. Get Ready for Work was introduced in response to the recommendations of the Beattie Committee (Scottish Executive, 1999a), which identified the need for more flexible and responsive training provision for young people with additional support needs. It is managed by the enterprise networks and it is delivered through Careers Scotland, local training providers and local enterprise companies (LECs). It is funded by Scottish Enterprise and Highlands and Islands Enterprise. Get Ready for Work primarily targets young people with additional support needs who are aged between 16 and 17. It replaced the Special Needs Skillseekers Programme and has four main strands – personal skills, life skills, vocational skills and core skills. Young people must be referred on to the programme by Careers Scotland. After an initial assessment of the young person's skills, aspirations and attitudes towards employment, the careers adviser will draw up an action plan. The training provider will then use this plan to draw up a training plan with goals for the young person to achieve. The programme is not time-limited, although the young person must leave when they are 18 unless there are good reasons why they should stay on the programme for longer. At the time of writing, Get Ready for Work was very new and there was no literature available that evaluated its effectiveness. However, a one-year evaluation of the programme was conducted internally by the Scottish Executive (unpublished). Although this evaluation was not available for public viewing, a representative from the Scottish Executive discussed the positive features of the programme which were highlighted by the evaluation:

> They are meeting and exceeding their targets of young people going through the programme, of young people progressing onto what we call positive outcomes, which are the jobs or the mainstream Skillseekers which is, you know, an employed job in a sense but still in a training programme or into further education. So I mean

> there is a success there and talking to various training providers it is beneficial and a lot of people are getting on it. (Representative, Beattie Implementation Team, Scottish Executive)

This quote suggests that although young people were coming onto Get Ready for Work in increasing numbers there was little evidence at that time to suggest that young people were finding paid jobs as a result of the programme. It is interesting that one of the indicators of success of the programme was to move people onto another mainstream training programme (Skillseekers). This may perpetuate the 'revolving door' image of trainees moving from one programme to another (see Riddell *et al.*, 2001 for a more detailed discussion). The Scottish Executive evaluation also highlighted some difficulties with the programme. In particular these related to the availability of the service and misunderstandings about the nature of the programme. These issues are also relevant to other training and employment programmes.

Misunderstanding the nature of the programme

There have been various interpretations around eligibility criteria for the programme. Young people who were not yet 'work-ready' had to be referred onto the programme by a careers adviser. Among service providers there appeared, in particular, to have been some doubt around age restrictions and time limitations for the programme. One provider, for example, asked young people to leave the course on their eighteenth birthday, while other providers may have been more flexible. Anecdotal evidence from the Scottish Executive suggested that some of the local enterprise companies put considerable pressure on training providers to get people off the programme and into a positive outcome (a job, a place on the Skillseekers programme or a further education placement) as quickly as possible. The nature of the difficulties and barriers faced by the particular group of young people in question means they are likely to need fairly intensive support over a relatively long period of time. This creates tensions, particularly around financial issues, and raises questions about responsibility. There appears to be a lack of clarity about what the overall goal of the programme is. Should the programme be aiming to find 'real', paid jobs for young people or should it simply attempt to provide work opportunities that offer young people experience and the opportunity to improve their 'employability'? This is a key dilemma that can be applied to many of the services in this area.

Availability of services by area

Another issue is the availability of services by area. Get Ready for Work is a relatively new programme and therefore it is perhaps understandable that development across the country has been patchy (Scottish Executive,

2003f). However, the availability of training and employment services generally would appear to differ according to geographical area (Riddell *et al.*, 2005). Clearly the lack of services in some areas, and the lack of providers offering particular services, will impact on the choices available to young people. The young people who are likely to make use of these programmes may be particularly limited as travelling to other areas where provision is available may not be an option for a variety of reasons such as an inability to travel independently. A lack of competition and choice of providers may also result in a lower quality of service. However, given that Get Ready for Work is a relatively new programme, it is too soon to say whether these inequalities by area will be permanent or will improve through time.

Need for greater flexibility

Although Get Ready for Work was introduced in order to provide more flexible employability training for young people with additional support needs, it would appear that even greater flexibility is needed. Some young people have not been ready for a work placement when referred on to Get Ready for Work, and they would have benefited from some additional training prior to this. Young people who have been assessed as not being 'work-ready' are referred onto Get Ready for Work, but this programme does not appear suitable for the 'least work-ready'. This is illustrated by the following quotes from a range of participants in the author's research:

> Get Ready for Work is a really good programme. We have had lots of successes of moving people into employment. However, I think there should be more flexibility with the programme. When a young person is referred to us, if we feel they are not yet ready to go out on placement then we don't have the resources to do anything else with them, we can't keep them behind for training for a few weeks, we don't have the resources to do it so we have to send them out anyway. The other thing that I think can be problematic is that young people have to be out on placement for 25–30 hours a week. This is too much for some of the young people. We cannot reduce the hours they work because they have to complete a timesheet each week. There is a real need for more flexibility across the board. (Employment development officer, voluntary organisation)

> There seems to be a bit of a gap for young people like Jamie basically who just needs that extra bit of support, you know, who has different needs and as I say is a bit more vulnerable and there is a bit of a gap in the provision that we have for that ... I feel that there is a gap in the provision, I really strongly feel there is a

> gap in the provision and I think that's something that needs to be addressed. Obviously that comes at a very high level, at a much higher level than I'm at ... It's difficult to find a placement for someone who is particularly vulnerable, that's a big issue that we have. (Social worker)

> It would have been good to have somebody to encourage me a wee bit more, somebody to get me to keep on going. It would have been nice to have somebody to talk to. (Imran, 20)

In a similar way to other employment programmes such as New Deal, Get Ready for Work appears to target those who are closer to the labour market, leaving a gap for the most vulnerable. It would appear that the common problem where young people (or other clients) have to fit in with existing services, rather than services being flexible enough to meet needs, continues to exist. There seems to be a contradiction between the policy rhetoric which suggests that all adults with a learning disability who want a job should be able to get one (Scottish Executive, 2000a) and the services that are available to provide the support required to achieve this. Despite the introduction of Get Ready for Work as a more flexible training programme for young people with additional support needs, even more imaginative and flexible approaches need to be adopted, as clearly this approach does not suit everyone.

Support to access employment

The Same As You? (Scottish Executive, 2000a) recommended that local authorities should put more effort into developing employment services for people with learning disabilities, and it was demonstrated that this could be cost-effective, as outlined in the previous chapter. Of course, these types of placement are time-limited and may only be suitable for those capable of progressing into open employment (Riddell *et al.*, 2005), but such was the commitment of the national review to expanding employment opportunities for people with learning disabilities, that a short-life working group on employment was established (Scottish Executive, 2003a).

The working group focused on the barriers faced by people with learning disabilities entering the labour market and recommended the changes that would be needed to reduce these barriers. The report recommended a fairer and simpler tax system as well as the promotion of non-discrimination and equality, suggesting that more changes are needed than simply providing employment services to assist disabled people into work. Key recommendations included the need for Jobcentre Plus to increase their efforts to engage with people with learning disabilities. In addition, Careers Scotland was to be more proactive in including people with learning disabilities in mainstream provision. Support should start at school, enabling people with learning disabilities to think about employment prospects from an earlier stage and allowing them to try part-time jobs (Scottish Executive, 2003a). The need for closer partnership working between local authorities, employers, voluntary organisations, trade unions, the Department for Work and Pensions, Careers Scotland, people with a learning disability and their families was identified as being crucial to taking the recommendations forward (Scottish Executive, 2003a). Figures from the Scottish Executive (2007a) suggest that some progress has been made in terms of developing employment opportunities for people with learning disabilities. In 2006, 3,712 adults with learning disabilities engaged in some sort of employment in Scotland. Only 29% of these were in open employment. The majority of those who worked did so for less than 15 hours per week (around 63%). A further 21% worked for 16–30 hours per week and the remaining 16% worked more than 30 hours per week (Scottish Executive, 2007a).

Glasgow City Council adopted many of the broad recommendations made by the short-life working group. This is illustrated in a consultation document published at the end of 2003 entitled *Equal Access to Employment* (Glasgow City Council, 2003). This document was produced to discuss the future of employment and vocational rehabilitation services for people with a range of health and social care needs within the city. The goal of the strategy was to ensure that:

> every adult in Glasgow regardless of age, gender, background, ethnicity, personal or health history should have the same opportunity as everyone else in the city to obtain and hold down meaningful and paid work. (Glasgow City Council, 2003, p. 1)

In order to achieve this goal it was recognised that an increased emphasis on partnership working between the public agencies, the voluntary sector and employers would be needed. People with health or social care needs would be enabled where possible to progress to real jobs in the labour market, offering the same employment conditions and opportunities for career enhancement enjoyed by the rest of the workforce. To enable this, the health and social care sector was to refocus its energies on realigning its resources to provide people with the health and social care support needed to enter and sustain employment rather than providing services in vocational and employment skills.

In parallel with the short-life working group, the consultation document recommended that wherever possible users of health and social care services should be moved to mainstream employment and training projects and these projects would be responsible for placing people in jobs. The document proposed the establishment of nine Equal Access Teams across the city, whose main role would be to bridge the gap between care managers and mainstream employment and training agencies. The Equal Access Teams would use the 'supported employment model' to help people access the labour market and sustain employment, although the level and nature of the support would vary according to the needs of each person (Glasgow City Council, 2003).

While a move towards mainstreaming should be regarded as broadly commendable, approaches such as the two outlined here do not appear to consider the ability of mainstream services to cope with the needs of people with health and social care needs seeking employment. Programmes such as Work Preparation or Training for Work that are offered by mainstream services are time-limited and are funded according to the outcomes that they achieve. As a result, they are likely to target their services at those people closest to the labour market. In an apparent contradiction to these recommendations, Jobcentre Plus has adopted a specialist approach to their Incapacity Benefit Pilots. This can be explained partly in terms of staff lacking the confidence to discuss employment issues with people with disabilities (see, for example, Thornton, 2003). While there is clearly an argument for the retraining of frontline staff to work more effectively with people with disabilities, there is also a need to recognise the potential difficulties in providing a service to meet the needs of those closest to the labour market as well as to those with more intensive support needs.

What has become clear from the discussion thus far is the increasing move towards improving employability for all sections of the population, using mainstream services where possible. The next section outlines briefly the mainstream services that are available to assist people with disabilities wishing to move into paid work.

The role of mainstream employment services in assisting people with disabilities into employment

New Deal for Disabled People

Stafford (2003) has described the New Deal for Disabled People (NDDP) as New Labour's main employment programme for people in receipt of Incapacity Benefit (IB). The programme was extended across the UK after a period of piloting in June 2001. There are now around 60 job brokers across Scotland: they are organisations from the not-for-profit public, private and voluntary sector, such as Capability Scotland. The role of the job broker is to work in close contact with the disabled person who will have been referred to them by a Disability Employment Adviser (DEA). The job broker will liaise with employers to secure a work placement for the person and will provide support and monitoring during the course of that placement.

The NDDP is an entirely voluntary programme and take-up has been relatively low at only 7% during the pilots (Stafford, 2003). Some clients did not take part because they were too ill but others, not identifying themselves as disabled, did not see the relevance of the programme for them. Levels of awareness of the scheme were also relatively modest, with only half of the eligible population having heard of the programme one year after it was extended UK-wide. In terms of employment outcomes, between July 2001 and September 2002 there were 27,850 registrations with job brokers: 22% of them had moved into employment, including 1,400 into sustainable employment. Again there is no way to be certain that these moves into employment would not have occurred anyway. Corden and colleagues (2003) found relatively high satisfaction among clients who had participated in the NDDP. Job brokers were often instrumental in raising client confidence and motivation through working on a one-to-one basis. However, clients' satisfaction tended to diminish when their expectations of the programme were unmet. In particular, clients tended to be disappointed in the level of proactiveness of job brokers in finding work for them (Corden *et al.*, 2003).

As discussed above, there was a tendency for participants on the programme to be closer to the labour market. During the pilot stages employment became the main programme outcome. This led to personal advisers only taking on those clients who were closest to the labour market. This is exacerbated by the funding regime for the national expansion, which has led some job brokers to prioritise those clients who were job-ready as they required less support and were more likely to generate an outcome-related payment (Stafford, 2003; Corden *et al.*, 2003). All of this raises questions for those who are further away from the labour market, and one of the main criticisms of the programme is that it does not offer enough support to those who are in greatest need.

Work Preparation Programme

Other employment programmes face similar dilemmas. One example is the Work Preparation Programme, which is Jobcentre Plus's main rehabilitation and retention programme. It is designed to develop capacity and confidence, overcome obstacles and explore alternative employment through short-term work trials (Riddell *et al.*, 2003). Training is not a core element of the programme, but it may include job-specific instruction which is necessary for a client to perform the tasks of the job. Like the NDDP, its budget is relatively modest and capped. In 2001/02, the budget allocated was £1.2 million (Riddell *et al.*, 2005). In 2002/03 expenditure on the NDDP was £30 million. By comparison, the budget for the New Deal for Lone Parents was £80 million and that for young people was £270 million (Stanley, 2003). This suggests that although the employment of people with disabilities is heralded as a high priority within policy rhetoric, this is not always matched in terms of funding.

Riddell and colleagues conducted an evaluation of the Work Preparation Programme (Riddell *et al.*, 2002, 2003). They found that people with physical disabilities accounted for the largest proportion of clients, while people with sensory impairments made up the smallest group. The length of placement ranged from one week to sixteen weeks, with a mean length of five weeks. Those categorised as having mental health problems tended to attend for two weeks or less, while the average placement for someone with a learning disability was on the whole longer.

In terms of employment outcomes, only 20% of people who participated gained employment at the end of the period, and for significant numbers there were subsequent problems with job retention (Riddell *et al.*, 2002). A further 12% required further education or training and 68% had unknown or unsuccessful outcomes (Riddell *et al.*, 2005). Of course, at first glance these outcomes appear relatively disappointing; however, much depends upon the definition of successful or unsuccessful outcome that have been used. These measures may not take into account soft outcomes such as increased self-confidence and therefore progress on these is not being measured. Riddell and colleagues (2002) encountered some confusion around what the purpose of work preparation was. Service users often believed that the purpose of work preparation was to get them into a job and were disappointed when this outcome was not achieved. Employers on the other hand were somewhat alarmed when they discovered that some service users were hoping for a job at the end of the placement (Riddell *et al.*, 2002).

Demand for the programme has increased, and in future priority may be given to those most likely to achieve a positive outcome within 13 weeks of completion and those who have not undertaken a work preparation programme within the last two years. This again creates dilemmas for service providers. Riddell *et al.* (2002, 2003) found differing views about which group should be targeted. Disability Service Team (DST) managers felt the service should be targeted at those closest to the labour market but there was a moral imperative not to turn away those with more significant impairments. It was suggested that two programmes might be developed, one for those people who were almost work-ready and one offering more intensive support for those unlikely to find work in the immediate future.

For those with more intensive needs, much longer than thirteen-week programmes are likely to be needed. Other programmes of significantly longer duration do exist within Scotland. Training for Work, funded by Scottish Enterprise and Highlands and Islands Enterprise, offers skills-based training, but it is not always possible for individuals to obtain places on these programmes due to high demand.

From the discussion of employment programmes, certain trends and dilemmas have become increasingly apparent. Most of the writers who have evaluated the programmes outlined above are in broad agreement that the programmes do not go far enough in terms of support offered to disabled people. The criticisms take a variety of forms including the fact that many of the programmes such as Work Preparation do not offer sufficient time to enable disabled people to establish themselves in the workplace. This may be attributed to funding mechanisms which put pressure on service providers to ensure quick turnover of clients, but it can also be linked to the fact that most employment programmes are supply-side measures.

The 1944 Disabled Persons (Employment) Act focused on the employment of disabled people and introduced the quota system whereby employers had to employ a certain percentage of disabled people as part of their workforce. Although the quota system was not taken seriously by many employers and few prosecutions were ever made, it was an excellent example of a demand-side measure where the onus was on the employer and workplace to change their practices and facilitate the employment of disabled people. The quota system was abolished with the introduction of the Disability Discrimination Act in 1995 and in recent years there has been a clear shift towards the supply-side measures outlined above. Supply-side measures focus on the deficits or perceived lack of work skills among disabled people and the task is to improve these to enable disabled people to fit in with the existing workplace. Despite the lip-service paid to social inclusion and the social model of disability, it is not clear how easily these supply-side measures sit alongside these. Barnes puts this well:

> over the years politicians and policy makers have adopted the language of inclusion and posited what at first glance seems like social model solutions to the problems associated with disability in the workplace, for example, the New Deal Programme and the DDA ... but policy remains largely centred on the supply rather than the demand side of labour ... policies which target and highlight functional limits of individuals with perceived impairments are prioritised and supported at the expense of those which draw attention to and seek to resolve the stark inequalities of the social organisation of work. (Barnes, 2003, p. 8)

Increasingly, disability writers are suggesting that in order for employment programmes to be successful in enabling people with disabilities to move into employment, they must go hand-in-hand with moves to reform the benefits system and make employment more financially attractive to disabled people (Bauman, 1988; Barnes, 2003). The New Labour government has pledged to move people off Incapacity Benefits where possible, and the introduction of the national minimum wage and Disabled Person's Tax Credit may be seen as a partial recognition of the need to make employment more financially attractive to disabled people.

The benefits system: help or hindrance?

Incapacity Benefit and other related benefits

The government at Westminster has laid out its plans to tackle the growing increase in Incapacity Benefit claimants in the Green Paper *Pathways to Work: Helping Disabled People into Employment* (Department for Work and Pensions, 2002), *A New Deal for Welfare: Empowering People to Work* (Department for Work and Pensions, 2006) and *In Work, Better Off* (Department for Work and Pensions, 2007). A House of Commons Select Committee set out the scale of the task, as the figures below show (Select Committee on Work and Pensions, 2003):

- Approximately half of disabled people in the UK were economically inactive, compared with 15% of the non-disabled population.
- In spring 2002 the employment rate for disabled people was 48% compared with an overall employment rate of 74.6%.
- In the last 20 years the number claiming Incapacity Benefit has trebled. There were 2.7 million incapacity-type claimants.
- In November 2002 there were 2.38 million Incapacity Benefit claimants and 45% of these had been on benefit for five years or more.
- The number of incapacity claimants dwarfed the number of unemployment benefit claimants, which is falling.
- Expenditure on Incapacity Benefit was over £16 billion, compared to £4 billion on Jobseeker's Allowance.

The problem is particularly significant in Glasgow, as highlighted by a project called The Glasgow Challenge (see McGregor *et al.*, 2003). The project found that within Glasgow some 90,000 of the jobless population were claiming a non-Jobseeker's Allowance key benefit such as Incapacity Benefit. These figures included 71,000 sick or disabled people and 17,000 lone parents. Key barriers to finding employment for this group were identified as poor physical health, poor mental health, physical disability, lack of childcare, benefits and debt issues, employer attitudes and behaviours, and issues around coping with work. Over half of those surveyed for the project reported five or more barriers (McGregor *et al.*, 2003). McGregor and colleagues argued that in order to address these barriers, significant gaps in services needed to be filled. These included the need to increase support around transitions into work and in-work, and making services for disabled people more work-focused.

In a bid to tackle some of these issues, the Green Paper (Department for Work and Pensions, 2002) focused on four key issues: increasing the frequency of work-focused interviews for new and recent IB claimants; providing a wider range of access to help to address key health- and non-health-related obstacles; improving financial incentives to enable clients to see that they are better off in work; and providing more support for people with health problems to move from incapacity-related benefits onto Jobseeker's Allowance. A programme to tackle these measures got underway in October 2003 in six Jobcentre Plus districts across the UK. These pilots extended the work-focused interview approach, making it compulsory to attend a number of work-related interviews to plan a route back to independence with a personal adviser. Other changes in the pilot areas included improved referral routes between these work-focused interviews and pre-existing sources of social support, the establishment of work-focused rehabilitation pilots in conjunction with the NHS, and new incentives to encourage recipients into work (Stanley, 2003). The pilots embraced a specialist approach and specialist Incapacity Benefit personal advisers were recruited. As mentioned at the beginning of the chapter, this appears to go against the mainstreaming approach of Jobcentre Plus (see Thornton, 2003). The argument appears to be that it is impossible for a generalist adviser to be sufficiently well-informed about medical conditions and their effects, the disability benefits system and the range of external specialist services. On the other hand, as Thornton points out:

> boosting the role of specialist advisors risks labelling the person as someone 'different' who needs 'special handling'. Strategies for attitudinal change among mainstream advisors, backed by working with disabled colleagues must be tried. (Thornton, 2003, p. 11)

In addition to this movement away from mainstreaming, the Green Paper was been criticised for 'not going far enough' (Stanley, 2003). It made little mention of employers and their responsibilities and how they might be supported in fulfilling them. This could be considered a weakness given that the report of the Glasgow Challenge Project (McGregor *et al.*, 2003) emphasises the key role for employers in assisting disabled people into employment. It can be argued the system is fundamentally flawed as a result of the continued emphasis on the dichotomy between those capable and incapable of work. Such rigid boundaries result in those being classified as 'incapable' having to take a considerable risk to move into employment. By doing so they are declaring themselves to be 'capable' and therefore no longer entitled to Incapacity Benefits (Select Committee on Work and Pensions, 2003; Schneider *et al.*, 2001).

There is a need to recognise a work continuum rather than a binary where people are able to work or not. Some limited attempts to do so can be seen in schemes such as the payment of £40 per week to Incapacity Benefit claimants if they return to work and are earning less than £15,000 per year. This additional payment is payable for 52 weeks and is designed to help IB claimants cope with the financial disruption of moving back into employment (Riddell *et al.*, 2005). The proposals outlined in the recent Green Paper *A New Deal for Welfare: Empowering People to Work* (Department for Work and Pensions, 2006) attempted to remove this dichotomy by transforming the Personal Capability Assessment process so that it focused on people's capacity to work rather than just their entitlements to benefits. There was to be a tailored, active system that addressed each individual's capacity rather than a model that writes people off as completely incapable of work. Those who were exempt were to be deemed so on the basis of the severity of the impact of their illness on their ability to function, rather than as the result of having a specific condition. In addition, general practitioners (GPs) and primary care teams were to be supported in the key role they play in helping people back to work. For those on existing benefits, the level of their benefits was to be protected should they enter work and find that they need to return to benefits (Department for Work and Pensions, 2006).

The Green Paper *In Work, Better Off* was published in July 2007 by the Department for Work and Pensions. It made more explicit the UK government's commitment to 'transform work and opportunity in Britain' (Department for Work and Pensions, 2007). The paper set out a series of measures to achieve full employment – a goal that is seen as central to the commitment to eradicate child poverty. A key measure was the establishment of Local Employment Partnerships, which aimed to encourage major employers in both the public and private sectors to create a quarter of a million job opportunities. These opportunities were to be targeted specifically at those who were disadvantaged in the labour market – including lone parents and those on Incapacity Benefit.

Anti-discrimination legislation

Disability Discrimination Act

As discussed in the previous section, employment services to assist disabled people into employment are unlikely to be effective unless they are accompanied by a reform of the benefits system. Likewise, in order to be used to greatest effect, employment services need to go hand-in-hand with anti-discrimination legislation. Part IV of the Disability Discrimination Act 1995 (DDA) extended the provisions of the Act to cover further and higher education institutions as well as local education authorities and local authorities in relation to adult education and youth services. In addition, from April 2004 the Act was extended to cover areas previously exempted from the employment provision, such as previously excluded occupations and small employers. New regulations (the Disability Discrimination Act 1995 (Amendment) Regulations 2003) announced in the Queens Speech in November 2003 placed a duty on public sector bodies to positively promote equality for disabled people in line with the Race Relations (Amendment) Act 2000.

The effectiveness of the DDA has been monitored closely by the Disability Rights Commission, and independent evaluations have been carried out. It would appear that awareness of the Act is growing and people are making increasing use of it. Meagre (2003) pointed out that cases being brought had steadily increased since the Act's inception in 1995, although the success rate for such cases was extremely low. The vast majority of cases were withdrawn or settled before they even reached court (Meagre, 2003). The Act would appear to be more successful in assisting those already in employment rather than those trying to move into the labour market. It is very difficult to prove that discrimination has occurred at the recruitment stage, and cases were less likely to be brought at that stage. There has been a slight increase in the employment rate of disabled people since the introduction of the Act, but it is very difficult to know whether this is attributable to the DDA or to other factors such as employment programmes (Riddell *et al.*, 2005).

The main criticism of the Act relates to the difficulties faced by people with disabilities both in meeting the definitions of disability under the Act and in proving that discrimination has occurred (Gooding, 2003). The onus is very much on the disabled person to prove not only that they are disabled (which can be difficult in the case of invisible disabilities) but also that discrimination has occurred as a result of their disability. Even when a disabled person can establish that they have been treated less favourably and as a result of their disability, there is a legal stipulation that the disability is sustained and long term (Roulstone, 2003). Claimants therefore have multiple hurdles to overcome in order to bring a successful claim under the Act. Even then employers may not be prosecuted if they can prove the discrimination was justified. The situation may improve, thought Gooding, as a result of the European Framework Directive which was due to come into effect in October 2004. This Directive stated that treatment against a disabled person could not be justified if it amounted to direct discrimination. This was defined as treating a disabled person less favourably on the grounds of their disability than a person not having that disability whose relevant circumstances were the same or not materially different from those of the disabled person (Gooding, 2003).

Most writers would appear to agree that the DDA has achieved some degree of success (Gooding, 2003; Meagre, 2003; Riddell *et al.*, 2005). However, by promoting equal opportunities the legislation may not do enough to enable some disabled people to access further education, training or employment and enjoy successful outcomes, however these may be defined. To access these areas, some people might need more than equal opportunities; those with more significant impairments may need extra support in the form of positive discrimination. To this end, demand-side rather than supply-side measures may be required.

Related to this anti-discrimination legislation is the introduction of the Equality Act which gained Royal Assent in 2006. The Act established the Commission for Equality and Human Rights, bringing together the Disability Rights Commission and the Equal Opportunities Commission from October 2007. The Commission for Racial Equality will join in 2009. The role of the Commission will be to work with individuals, communities, businesses and public services to find new and more effective ways to combat discrimination. It is relatively early at this point to speculate as to the likely impact of these changes on the lives of people with learning disabilities.

The advantages and disadvantages of supported employment

A review of the relevant policy documents relating to learning disability and employment suggests that all share a common feature: they regard supported employment as the optimum support mechanism to enable people with learning disabilities to move into and sustain paid employment. Supported employment can take various forms. The principle of supported employment in its true sense involves placement in open employment with guidance, support and feedback from a job coach or a member of staff (Schneider, 1998a; see also O'Bryan *et al.*, 2000; Wilson; 2003). Job tasks are broken down into small component parts to allow the person with learning disability to master the job (Wilson, 2003). Generally it is hoped that the job coach will eventually withdraw, leaving the person with learning disabilities to work with natural support from work colleagues. The most crucial element of supported employment in the true sense is that the person with learning disabilities or other support needs is paid for the work that they do, hence the slogan 'real pay for real work' (Wilson, 2003). There are variations on this true supported employment model, with various training schemes and work placements adopting similar methods (although the supported employee/trainee is unlikely to be paid a real wage in these cases). (See Riddell *et al.*, 2005, for a more detailed discussion of employment schemes available). At present, access to supported employment remains limited. There is an overall shortage of supported employment places but there is also marked geographical variation in terms of availability (O'Bryan *et al.*, 2000).

Careers Scotland established eight supported employment pilot projects in Scotland, which have recently been evaluated. The evaluation found that, despite initial delays, good progress had been made in developing innovative models of practice at local levels (Scottish Executive, 2003g). However, it would appear that there was still a lack of understanding overall about supported employment and the role of the pilots in particular. At the time of the evaluation the programme was significantly below its anticipated target outcome levels, although these were likely to be reviewed. This may be due in part to the late start dates of many of the projects. However, another possible reason may be the concept of 'job-readiness' (Scottish Executive, 2003g). The original guidance provided by the Scottish Executive Enterprise, Transport and Lifelong Learning Department (SEETLLD) explained that clients receiving support were expected to be nearly 'job-ready'. The evaluation found a number of instances where client were far from job-ready. This may stem from a lack of understanding around the concept of job-readiness, but may also arise from ethical issues around turning clients away. This represents a crucial dilemma for service providers in terms of the client group to be targeted. The report, although highlighting some instances of success, would appear to raise some questions about the appropriateness of the supported employment model for young people with additional support needs.

A later report evaluating the pilots, published by the Scottish Executive in 2005 (Scottish Executive, 2005d), painted a broadly similar picture. The projects continued to perform below their targets as a result of delays in getting started and a lack of clarity around the definition of job-readiness, which often resulted in inappropriate referrals being made. In 2003/04 a total of 342 clients had participated with 146 entering a supported employment opportunity of which 90 had sustained for three months or longer (Scottish Executive, 2005d). At first glance these figures do not appear particularly encouraging, but there are wider benefits such as an improvement in terms of soft and vocational skills and a better understanding of the world of work.

The research on supported employment for adults with a range of disabilities presents a mixed view of the relative advantages and disadvantages. The US literature on supported employment for people with a range of intellectual disabilities paints a positive picture. Overall, in the USA, it appears that supported employment for adults with severe as well as mild and moderate intellectual impairments brings benefits in a number of areas. Participants are significantly better off in supported employment than on welfare benefits (Wehman and Kregel, 1995). Supported employees earn around double the hourly pay rate found in sheltered workshops (Beyer and Kilsby, 1996a). In addition they have enjoyed an enhanced quality of life as a result of increased interaction with other members of the community (Wehman and Kregel, 1995). (See also Parent *et al.*, 1991; Kregel, 1997; Mank *et al.*, 1997).

Research in the UK, however, has painted a slightly less convincing picture of the benefits of supported employment for adults with learning disabilities. On a positive note, Bass and Drewett (1997) found that supported employment was valued by supported employees and employers alike (see also Weston, 2002). In particular, the support provided by job coaches was valued, although there was evidence to suggest that natural support systems could be developed earlier in the process (Bass and Drewett, 1997). Indeed, Roulstone *et al.* (2002) found that informal support from colleagues was particularly important for disabled workers. The author's research suggested that the levels of support experienced were inadequate, as the following quote suggests:

> There has been no contact at all. I don't even have a contact name of someone I could get in touch with if there was a problem. I have worked with different schemes in the past and there has always been a link person for me to get in touch with. But this project doesn't seem to have anything along those lines. (Employer, retail)

Riddell *et al.* (1999), drawing on data from the ESRC project 'The Meaning of the Learning Society for Adults with Learning Difficulties' suggested that the economic benefits of supported employment in Scotland (and the rest of the UK) are only marginal. Among three case studies highlighted, only one man, who spent 60% of his week in supported employment, was significantly better off (Riddell *et al.*, 2001). A lack of experience and qualifications means that employees have to go for entry level jobs with low hourly rates of pay (Beyer and Kilsby, 1996a). In addition, many supported employees spend only a small proportion of their week in employment, as the most recent figures from the Scottish Executive outlined above suggest (Scottish Executive, 2007a). This can be attributed in part to the restrictions imposed by the benefits system (Beyer and Kilsby, 1996b; O'Bryan *et al.*, 2000). The evidence suggests that increased levels of vocational integration are associated with increased presence of people with disabilities within the workplace (Walsh and Linehan, 1997). Those supported employees who work longer hours each week have greater opportunities to attend staff meetings, follow a work schedule similar to the majority of their co-workers and earn wages comparable to their co-workers (Walsh and Linehan, 1997). In addition, they are likely to enjoy greater social interaction. In the author's own research, young people tended to be excluded from social activities as a result of working fewer hours than their colleagues.

The quality of the social interaction experienced by British supported employees has been called into question. Riddell *et al.* (2001) found that, although each person in their study valued their job highly, the social relationships they had created were superficial and did not extend beyond the working day (Riddell *et al.*, 2001). The type of interaction experienced is often different to that of non-disabled colleagues. Supported employees were found to be recipients of more befriending, training and information-giving than their non-disabled counterparts (Beyer and Kilsby, 1996a). In addition, they were found to receive superficial interaction such as praise and greetings more frequently than non-disabled colleagues and were much less involved in workplace banter such as teasing or joking. Interestingly, a study that compared the cost-effectiveness of a special needs unit with a supported employment project for people with severe intellectual disabilities and high support needs, found that those on the supported employment project had greater social contact with people outside social services but had less social involvement overall (Shearn *et al.*, 2000).

Wilson (2003) has identified the principle of 'real jobs' as one of the key difficulties with the supported employment model. The principle of 'real jobs' is underpinned by the principles of normalisation and integration. This has resulted in reluctance among job coaches and other voluntary agency staff as well as employers to change components of the job to better meet the abilities of the supported employee. Instead, the onus is on the supported employee to develop the skills required to complete the tasks to a satisfactory level, often resulting in the breakdown of the placement. Wilson advocates a more careful appreciation of the nature and consequences of impairment in the work situation:

> it is clear that many voluntary organisations are perhaps complicit in discriminating against people with cognitive impairments by not questioning the criteria of a 'real job' and making sufficient reasonable adjustments to such criteria to enable individuals to work ... successful inclusion rests upon the proper restructuring of the tasks they [supported employees] are required to complete. (Wilson, 2003, p. 114)

It is clear that supported employment as a model offers many benefits for people with disabilities who wish to make the transition to work, but some of these benefits may have been overstated, particularly in the American literature. Despite this, supported employment continues to be regarded as a panacea by British policy makers. There would appear to be an assumption among policy makers that supported employment is a part of the process of transition to work and that people with disabilities will eventually be able to work without support in 'real jobs'. However, as Wilson (2003) has pointed out, this might not be the case, particularly if employers and voluntary organisations are reluctant to make reasonable adjustments as a result of a perhaps misguided commitment to the principles of normalisation and integration. Jones *et al.* (2002) have some concerns that progression into open employment may not be possible in every case, particularly for those with more severe impairments. As a result they advocate the availability of support at crucial times in every supported employee's career. It would appear therefore that a balance needs to be struck between ensuring a throughput from services (where the supported employee is capable and wants to move on) and at the same time ensuring enough support for each supported employee's unique progression (Taylor *et al.*, 2004). Hyde (1998) has suggested that problems relating to progression from supported employment into open employment may relate to the contradictory aims of the model: supported employment aims to provide a supportive environment for workers with low productivity, while at the same time integrating disabled people into mainstream employment. Supported employment alone cannot facilitate the inclusion of disabled people into the workplace. Developments in this area must be underpinned by non-punitive, progressive social welfare policies and anti-discrimination legislation (discussed above) (Gosling and Cotterill, 2000). In addition, consideration must be given to alternatives for those for whom employment remains an unrealistic option.

Discussion

Both the Scottish Executive and UK government have presented a clear policy message that all people with learning disabilities should have paid employment if they want it. In order to achieve this goal, people with learning disabilities require access to adequate support services. This is a complex area and there are a wide range of services available. This chapter has attempted to unpack some of this complexity, providing an overview of the services and discussing their effectiveness or otherwise. The availability of services can vary by locality as different local authority areas may have different priorities. Although theoretically a wide range of services should result in greater choice, in actual fact the result can often be confusion for people with learning disabilities and their families, with different service providers offering similar, often overlapping projects and programmes. In addition, despite the number of programmes available these often do not meet the needs of people with learning disabilities.

Crucially, research has shown that people with learning disabilities need long term, often intensive support in order to sustain employment. The model of supported employment (which is currently regarded as the panacea) as it currently stands does not provide adequate support to enable many people with learning disabilities to sustain an employment place. Programmes which have to meet specified targets in order to continue to be financed are unlikely to be appropriate providers of long-term support.

Projects such as these are likely to focus on those closest to the labour market in order to demonstrate that they are a successful intervention. People with greater and long-term support needs are not an attractive option for providers. The Get Ready for Work programme is an example of a service which, although introduced to create greater flexibility, is still not flexible enough to meet the needs of those furthest from the labour market. Indeed, there is a gap in terms of service provision for people who need greater support. This raises questions about what the overall goal of services should be – should they be about assisting people with learning disabilities to find real, paid work, or are they simply providing people with experience in order to improve their employability?

In addition, the whole notion of employment as the route out of social exclusion for people with learning disabilities needs to problematised. A survey conducted by the Scottish Consortium for Learning Disability in 2006 (Curtice, 2006), found that employment did not feature highly in the list of things that mattered most to people with learning disabilities (these being getting their own home, having friends and being able to go out more). Only one in three respondents were currently working, and of those who did not work only 35% wanted to work: 48% did not want to work and 17% were unsure. In addition, given that the majority of those who are working do so for less than 16 hours each week (Scottish Executive, 2007a), people with learning disabilities who are in paid employment are unlikely to be financially better off.

This raises the question as to whether employment does result in greater social inclusion for people with learning disabilities. The author's own research has shown that people with learning disabilities who do work are likely to be found in poorly paid, routine and mundane jobs. These jobs rarely meet the expectations of people with learning disabilities. In addition, given the limited number of hours people are able to work, usually as a result of the benefits trap, people are likely to be excluded from important workplace roles and tasks, including social activities. This is not to deny the overall value and positive aspects of employment for those who successfully find and sustain it, but a note of caution and realism is required when considering employment opportunities for people with learning disabilities.

CHAPTER 4

Promoting Health and Well-being

Literature on employment has highlighted its health benefits in terms of overall mental health and well-being. Warr (1994), for example, has written about the benefits of employment and has highlighted the negative consequences of unemployment for adults (see also Warr, 1983, 1987). Employment is thought to produce personal and health benefits and it can have a positive impact on self-esteem, income, social relationships and leisure activities (Huxley, 2001). It is also clear that unemployment causes a decrement in mental health. It increases the risk of suicide and also the use of mental health services (Huxley, 2001). Yet, according to Schneider (1998b), working for anything other than financial gain is a little understood concept within capitalist societies. For example, volunteering can not only be a means to finding paid employment but can also generate social contacts and friendships. In addition, it can bring opportunities to make a social contribution and challenge some of the negative stereotypes of disabled people as passive recipients of care. Despite its benefits (Corden and Ellis, 2004), however, volunteering has not been fully exploited in Britain. Clearly the benefits of work extend beyond financial gain. However, the picture is not straightforward, and Warr (1994) pointed out that the range of mental health scores was very wide among both employed and unemployed people. Indeed, in a minority of cases unemployment can give rise to better mental health than certain forms of employment – jobs which are highly stressful, for example. There are some negative aspects to employment that have been identified in the previous chapter. According to Schneider (1998b), competition for jobs and the risk of failure can be damaging for an individual's mental health.

The general health and well-being of people with learning disabilities is the focus of this chapter. Scottish policy is explicitly committed to social inclusion and tackling inequality. Supporting people with health needs is an essential contribution towards achieving inclusion and social justice. There is an aim to improve health and life expectancy for all of the population, but particularly those from disadvantaged communities (NHS Health Scotland, 2004). This chapter will begin by outlining the general and more specific health needs of people with learning disabilities. It will identify the barriers that adults with learning disabilities face in having these needs met and will assess the potential impact of current policies and services in meeting these needs. The chapter will look critically at the ongoing debate around the extent to which specialist workers such as community learning disability nurses are required to enable adults with learning disabilities to have their health needs met, and the extent to which this role can be performed by generic health care staff. The chapter will conclude by looking briefly at the potential of more recent policies that take a more proactive approach in promoting good health and well-being among this client group.

What are the health needs of people with learning disabilities?

People with learning disabilities have similar health needs to the general population. Research has shown, however, that they have a higher number of health needs, more complex health needs and a greater number of unmet health needs. People with learning disabilities present with a different pattern of health needs and their causes of death are also different from those of the general population (see, for example, Beange *et al.*, 1995; Kerr, 1998, 2004). Respiratory disease is the main cause of death in people with learning disabilities. They are at risk of respiratory tract infections caused by aspiration or reflux if they have swallowing difficulties and they are less likely to be immunised against infections. Coronary heart disease is the second highest cause of death in people with learning disabilities (Royal College of Nursing, 2006). People with particular syndromes also have specific health needs associated with these conditions. Those with downs syndrome, for example, are more likely to experience congenital heart problems, dementia and thyroid problems.

Among people with learning disabilities generally, the prevalence of mental health problems is higher than among those without: they are twice as likely to experience mental health problems at some point in their life, and three times more likely to experience schizophrenia (Royal College of Nursing, 2006). There is also a greater prevalence of epilepsy than for the general population: one third of people with learning disabilities have the condition compared with 1% of the general population. The prevalence increases with the severity of learning disabilities, and nearly half of people with severe learning disabilities have epilepsy (Royal College of Nursing, 2006). People with learning disabilities also have much higher rates (roughly double) of gastro-intestinal cancers and other gastro-intestinal disorders such as helicobacter pylori, gastro-intestinal reflux disease, constipation and coeliac disease (Royal College of Nursing, 2006).

In terms of health promotion, uptake of screening for particular conditions tends to be lower among people with learning disabilities. For example, take-up rates for smear tests to detect cervical cancer among females are very low for people with learning disabilities. This may be due in part to assumptions made about the sexuality of women with learning disabilities both by the medical profession and by carers. People with learning disabilities are more likely to have tooth decay, loose teeth, gum disease, higher levels of untreated mouth disease and a larger number of tooth extractions. This may be explained by poor diet and poor dental hygiene and because the promotion of oral health may not be accessible to people with learning disabilities. Similarly, people with learning disabilities are more likely to develop hypertension and obesity and to lack exercise (Royal College of Nursing, 2006). This is likely to have a knock-on effect and lead to the development of conditions such as heart disease and type two diabetes. It should be borne in mind, however, that it is not clear how far ethnicity and wider cultural, economic and other factors impinge on the health profile of people with learning disabilities. Despite the additional health needs identified for this population, and the complexity that often accompanies these problems, people with learning disabilities tend to access health care less frequently than the general population (Scottish Executive, 2000a).

Research conducted by a team of researchers at Glasgow University and funded by the Chief Scientist Office of the Scottish Executive (Curtice *et al.*, 2001a) identified a number of barriers faced by people with learning disabilities in meeting their health needs. The research had two aims: firstly to ascertain perceptions of the health needs of people with learning disabilities living in the community, and secondly to ascertain obstacles to the identification and management of health needs. The research was conducted in two phases. Phase one involved carrying out 21 focus groups with people with learning disabilities, carers, and health and social care professionals. The second phase involved conducting in-depth interviews with people with learning disabilities and their carers about their lived experiences. In addition, the GP notes and social work notes of the participants with learning disabilities were reviewed for a one-year period in order to identify the level of communication and information sharing that occurred between GPs and social workers.

The research highlighted a number of barriers that existed for people with learning disabilities when accessing primary health care. This is supported by previous and subsequent research. The research findings differed from those of other studies, however, in that rather than visiting the GP less often, participants in this study visited their GP more regularly. Their use of the GP service was not very effective, however, and there was evidence of multiple visits to address routine health conditions which had perhaps been misdiagnosed on previous visits. One of the key difficulties identified for people with learning disabilities was lengthy waiting times often experienced at the GP surgery. This made a visit to the GP traumatic both for the person with learning disabilities and, at times, for their carer. Communication issues meant that the standard appointment time offered by GPs was often insufficient for people with learning disabilities to have their health needs dealt with. The research found that people with learning disabilities did not feel comfortable when communicating with professionals such as GPs. This was exacerbated by the discomfort felt by some GPs questioned, who did not feel able to communicate well with people with learning disabilities. This may have stemmed in part from a lack of training for medical students in working with people with learning disabilities at the early stages of their medical careers (Scottish Executive, 2000a). In addition, those people with learning disabilities who lived with paid carers rather than family carers often experienced difficulties when the member of staff who supported them to attend the GP was unfamiliar with the particular medical issue in question.

Primary care generally tends to offer a largely reactive, rather than proactive, service, which seems to be unhelpful to people with learning disabilities. The research found that people with learning disabilities often experienced difficulty in following up health issues and required additional support to do this. If they required test results, for example, or a follow-up appointment to check whether or not a particular treatment had worked, it was unlikely that the primary care team would follow this up. People with learning disabilities require support to follow through their medical treatment or care. The research also identified a lack of co-ordination when someone needed input from different professionals or departments.

The research recommended that responsibility for meeting the health needs of people with learning disabilities should occur at all levels. People should be empowered to take responsibility for their own health needs alongside support being made available for carers to assist in this matter, possibly via training and, in the case of paid carers, by making better use of hand-held health logs, for example. The research recommended that GPs and the primary care team should have responsibility for the health needs of people with learning disabilities, with access to specialist support from community learning disability teams where this was appropriate. This fits in broadly with current policy recommendations.

Current policy on the health of people with learning disabilities

The Same As You? (Scottish Executive, 2000a) pointed out that a GP practice with 1,500 patients can expect to have 22 to 30 people with mild learning disabilities and up to six people with severe disabilities. Therefore the review recommended that primary health care teams work to develop better links with community learning disability teams, suggesting that GPs and specialists both have a role to play:

> Many people will be able to use general community and hospital based services for specific treatment. Some people with learning

> disabilities will need support to use these services. Children and adults with extra and complex needs will need ongoing services from a range of PAMs [Professions Allied to Medicine] linked to community learning disability services. (Scottish Executive, 2000a, p. 87)

The review recognised the important role of professions allied to medicine (PAMs), including physiotherapists, occupational therapists, speech and language therapists, chiropodists and dieticians, in ensuring the health needs of people with learning disabilities were met (Scottish Executive, 2000a). It recognised that those with complex needs would need additional support.

Alongside the recommendations made in *The Same As You?*, which related specifically to health, the White Paper *Towards a Healthier Scotland* was published in 1999 (Scottish Executive, 1999b). This White Paper made recommendations to improve the health of the nation generally but made a small number of recommendations relating specifically to the health of people with learning disabilities. It proposed that health inequalities be tackled at three levels. Level one involved improving life circumstances such as social inclusion, income, education, and environmental factors which impact on health. Factors such as poverty and social exclusion were highlighted as having an indirect impact on health. Level two involved tackling aspects of lifestyles such as poor diet and lack of exercise (which can be a common problem among people with learning disabilities) and tobacco and alcohol consumption. Level three involved carrying out direct work to tackle diseases that can be prevented, such as heart diseases and cancers (Scottish Executive, 1999b). In England and Wales, the *Health of the Nation Strategy* (Department of Health, 1992) identified five key areas for health improvement. For people with learning disabilities, the focus on cardiovascular disease and cancers is particularly relevant, as a high proportion of people with learning disabilities carry one or more risk factors associated with morbidity and mortality from these causes (Turner and Moss, 1996). However, Turner and Moss argue that other health needs outlined above that are common in this group should not be overlooked as a result of such generic strategies or health promotion campaigns.

In addition to this, in 2003 the Scottish Executive published *Promoting Health, Supporting Inclusion: The National Review of the Contribution of All Nurses and Midwives to the Care and Support of People with Learning Disabilities* (Scottish Executive, 2003h). The review recommended a tiered approach to care, with a person able to access services at different tiers at different times according to changing needs. Tier 0 included community resources and supports, housing and support packages, education and learning, employment, public health initiatives and policy development.

Tier 1 was primary health care services that are directly accessed, as well as paid and family carers. Tier 2 was generic secondary (outpatient, inpatient and domiciliary) health services accessed via primary care services. Tier 3 was specialist learning disability services provided by local authorities, NHS Scotland and the independent sector. Finally, tier 4 was supra-specialist (tertiary) learning disability services provided by the local authority, NHS Scotland and the independent sector.

In response to this, the Health Needs Assessment report was published by NHS Health Scotland in 2004. The Health Needs Assessment found evidence of overt and more subtle unintentional discrimination within NHS Scotland towards people with learning disabilities. Examples included health professionals assuming that the most interventionist treatments such as intensive care, surgery, transplants and resuscitation should not be offered to someone with learning disabilities, and clinical guidelines failing to consider the impact their implementation would have on people with learning disabilities (NHS Health Scotland, 2004). The report made 25 recommendations in order to improve health and reduce inequality. It identified that action was required in five key areas: leadership and accountability, infrastructure, specialist interventions, information and education.

The report recommended that the Scottish Executive should take responsibility for ensuring national action to improve the health of people with learning disabilities. In addition, local databases of people with learning disabilities were to be established and a programme of research into the health needs of people with learning disabilities was to be funded by the Scottish Executive. The report also recommended that funding be made available to the Scottish Consortium for Learning Disabilities and NHS Scotland in order that they might identify, evaluate, promote and disseminate health improvement information and co-ordinate initiatives across Scotland. People with learning disabilities who are from ethnic minority communities, asylum seekers, refugees or members of the homeless community required particular attention. It was also suggested that the needs of people with learning disabilities should be included in the induction of all new NHS staff. It was recommended that NHS Education for Scotland should expand its work with the Scottish Consortium for Learning Disabilities to review and develop the learning disabilities component of all pre-registration health professionals' training programmes. In addition, learning disabilities modules should be included within post-qualifying and postgraduate programmes.

Health checks for people with learning disabilities

A common feature of the policy documentation discussed here is the recommendation that health checks should be made available to people with learning disabilities. The Health Needs Assessment recommended that:

> A specific health screening programme for people with learning disabilities should be established and implemented locally to a set of national standards. Local responsibility should lie with the Learning Disabilities Forum and Community Health Partnership ... in addition, person centred health management should be in place locally for each person with learning disabilities from a named worker who is responsible for actioning recommendations from the health screen. (NHS Health Scotland, 2004, p. 9)

The notion of providing a health check for people with learning disabilities would appear to make sense, given the large proportion of unmet health needs identified as a problem for this group. Within the Glasgow area health checks were introduced after the reconfiguration of community learning disability teams. A primary care liaison team was established to work across the city. This team consisted of learning disability nurses, doctors and a health promotion officer. In addition to carrying out health checks, the main roles of this team were to facilitate access to primary care for people with learning disabilities in the city, and to provide information and training for primary care professionals. The team was also responsible for creating a database to inform GPs of the number of people with learning disabilities that were registered with them, as well as carrying out research.

The health check instrument used in Glasgow was the 21st Century Health Check. This was developed at the University Affiliated Programme at the University of Glasgow and was adapted from an instrument developed by Lennox in Australia. The check comprised a review of GP records, a detailed history, and a selected physical examination including a urine test, a hearing test and blood tests where indicated. The results of the check were notified to the person and their carer and the GP, with indications as to referrals suggested as a result of the check.

The health check was piloted and evaluated before being rolled out across the city. Forty-seven people with learning disabilities took part in the pilot study. The health needs which were known about prior to the health check were identified from GP records. The most common were mental health problems (45), diseases of the nervous system (33), diseases of the digestive system (30) and diseases of the musculo-skeletal system and connective tissue (21). A total of 283 known health needs were identified in the 47 individuals. Of the 47 people, 43 were receiving prescribed drugs (there was a mean of five prescribed drugs). In the 12 months before the check the number of GP consultations per individual ranged from zero to 29 (Curtice *et al.*, 2001b).

The outcomes of the health checks indicated a high level of unmet need. Eighty outstanding screens or immunisations were identified, including

38 polio and 31 tetanus boosters. There were 49 further investigations deemed necessary, including hearing assessments (10), vision screening (7) and blood monitoring (11). In addition, 125 health needs or symptoms were identified for which assessment or intervention was considered necessary. These included newly identified needs and conditions that were known about but were not being managed optimally. Among the new needs identified were 17 reviews of medication and 19 instances of health promotion advice including dietary advice and support. The checks generated 156 recommendations. Of these, 40 were to a practice nurse, 36 were to GPs and 14 to (community learning disability) dieticians. Twelve individuals required co-ordination that in future could be provided by a nurse care manager (Curtice *et al.*, 2001b).

The views of GPs, carers and people with learning disabilities were sought about the health checks. Out of 37 GPs, 23 felt that people with learning disabilities required longer appointment times. They also identified a need for more information and training about learning disability. Carers broadly valued the health check. Of 37 carers questioned, 31 said that the person they cared for had been comfortable during the health check. Interviews about the process were carried out with 32 of the 47 people with learning disabilities who received a health check. Only two people who took part said that they felt uncomfortable during the process. People liked having the check at home and found the relationship with the nurse to be positive. They did not like spending a lot of time filling in forms and some people found some of the questions to be intrusive. People felt that it was important for them to receive feedback after the health check. The nurses who carried out the health checks were also interviewed. They felt that they had learned new skills in order to conduct the checks. As trained learning disability nurses, they were able to find ways to engage with people during the check. Carrying out the checks represented a change of role for them – they felt more actively involved in making a difference to the person's health but less directly involved in following up problems.

The evaluation concluded that it was both feasible and acceptable for specialist nurses to conduct health checks (Curtice *et al.*, 2001b). The checks provided the opportunity for more active management of health needs as well as providing a sound evidence base for service planning. The evaluation recommended that health checks be rolled out across primary care and community services for people with learning disabilities on the basis of the pilot. The research also recommended further development of protocols for health gain and service co-ordination to build on this foundation (Curtice *et al.*, 2001b). This concurs with other research in the field. For example, Martin *et al.* (1997) found that one year after a health check had been conducted, people with learning disabilities experienced significant health gains with regard to physical conditions. In contrast, mental health problems were under-reported and participants had achieved few gains on follow up (see also Barr *et al.*, 1999).

Examples of good practice across Scotland

Measures to improve the health needs of people with learning disabilities have been implemented in different ways across the country and progress has been patchy. Local agencies were asked to set out in their Partnership in Practice agreements for 2004–2007 their plans for addressing health promotion and improving access to health services generally for people with learning disabilities. Few local authorities had clear targets and timescales to deliver their proposals (Scottish Executive, 2007a). There were, however, some examples of good practice, as the summary table below shows.

Table 4.1 Good practice examples

Local authority	Good practice
Aberdeen/ Aberdeenshire	Specialist health promotion post for mental health Plan to develop a local learning disability health improvement strategy
Borders	Programme of health assessments developed by community learning disability nurses in selected practices in collaboration with GPs and practice nurses, with the hope that primary care staff would take ongoing responsibility for health assessments and screening
Western Isles	Developments in community nursing Consultant medical post created Good links with primary care and GP services
Dumfries and Galloway	Local research undertaken in 2003 Health promotion strategy being developed for completion in March 2005, including screening Community learning disability teams being established as part of the joint learning disability service, aiming to build strong links with primary and secondary care providers
Dundee City	Progress on healthy living and lifestyles materials in accessible format Joint health improvement plan that includes the needs of people with learning disabilities, with specific health promotion initiatives targeted at this group
East Ayrshire	Development of a CHIP (Community Health Improvement Partnership) mobile healthy living centre which includes people with learning disabilities in its activities
Fife	Creation of a new hospital liaison nursing post funded from the Change Fund

Local authority	Good practice
East Renfrewshire	Research project supported, looking at the service needs of individuals with learning disabilities and/or dementia Plan to build on the results to promote early recognition, assessment and appropriate service responses
Forth Valley	Priorities for service improvement focused on: – access to acute general hospital services including the development of a communications pathway and improved clinical practice – access to primary care including the provision of support and training to frontline staff, and – a well man clinic Learning disability nurse appointed for six months to develop training and awareness-raising for primary care staff. The appointment of a dedicated disability adviser led to environmental adaptations and staff training GP specialist in learning disabilities appointed, which improved information available to primary care services
Highland	Partners in the Health and Happiness initiative run by people with a learning disability to break down the barriers they face to achieving health and happiness. Through this initiative they work together to help people with a learning disability to speak up for what matters to them and find answers for the difficulties they face such as accessing supports and leisure or finding suitable jobs
Inverclyde	Clear recognition given to the development of health priorities including forensic learning disability service, an acute hospital liaison post, primary care liaison and support, a health checks project In relation to health promotion, reviewing resources and looking at information and training on sexual health and blood-borne viruses
South Ayrshire	Progress in a number of areas including the introduction of a fast-track information scheme operating within the acute hospitals in Ayrshire to ensure people with a learning disability have a quicker, smoother admission Piloting of a Personal Health Record to provide a user-friendly source of health information that service users and carers can take to appointments with GPs and other health care professionals
Grampian	Liaison health visitors appointed to support young people with learning disabilities and to provide a link between primary care and specialist settings Community learning disability teams in Moray and Aberdeenshire, providing support and training for staff in general health settings to enable people with learning disabilities to access services in local hospitals and other settings

Discussion

In order to promote social inclusion and allow people to develop social capital, people must be able to access services which ensure that their health needs are being met and their overall well-being is being promoted. This can be done through a variety of mechanisms, including health promotion, access to valued daily activities such as education and employment, and access to community facilities and leisure opportunities. This chapter has shown that people with learning disabilities are no different in this respect. What is clear, however, is that people with learning disabilities generally experience more significant health problems – and a greater number of them – than the general population, and are likely to have greater unmet health needs. Paradoxically this is a group who tend to access services less often. This is particularly true in relation to health promotion and screening activities.

The overall policy directive is clear: people with learning disabilities should have the majority of their health needs met by mainstream services, with appropriate access to specialist services where necessary. In order to deal with the issue of unmet health needs, health checks have been promoted as a means by which new health needs can be identified and then managed. Different local authority and health board areas have adopted different approaches to this. Areas such as Dumfries and Galloway have created new community learning disability teams whose main role is to ensure that people with learning disabilities have their health needs met. Glasgow, on the other hand, has disbanded its community learning disability teams, putting resources instead into the development of a primary care liaison team whose main role is to ensure unmet health needs are addressed via health checks and improving access to mainstream services.

The debate around the suitability of generic or specialist services to meet the health needs of people with learning disabilities is likely to continue. In social inclusion terms, ensuring people with learning disabilities have access to mainstream health services is clearly crucial. It should be borne in mind however that, as in the field of further education, people with learning disabilities are financially attractive to service providers. General practices receive an enhanced payment for each patient who has been classified as having a learning disability. While this can be viewed as a positive recognition of the greater needs of patients with learning disabilities, practices must ensure that the services they provide are more flexible and accessible.

People with learning disabilities require additional support in order to access health services. They need to be empowered to manage their own health where possible and to make informed choices about their health, particularly in relation to health promotion and lifestyle choices (see, for example, Young and Chesson, 2008). Research has suggested that there is a valuable job to be done in assisting people with learning disabilities to navigate their way around different health services. In particular, people with learning disabilities might benefit from support which enables them to take a more proactive approach to their health. Services which are currently reactive rather than proactive are not in the best position to do this. Assistance in terms of co-ordinating services is invaluable. This is the area to which the next chapter will turn.

CHAPTER 5

Co-ordinating Service Provision

The preceding chapters have shown the ways in which policies and services have changed for people with learning disabilities in recent years. A common theme running throughout the book is the drive to provide increasingly flexible and individualised services in order to enable people with learning disabilities to access appropriate education and employment opportunities as well as health services. The result has been the development of a complex maze of services which people may need support to negotiate. This chapter looks at the role of social work in empowering people to access appropriate services and support.

The changing nature of social work

Social work and the role of the social worker in Scotland have been under the spotlight as a result of a number of high profile cases with tragic results such as the abuse of a woman with learning disabilities, known only as Miss X, by her carers in the Scottish Borders. As in other cases like this, the public perception was that social work was to blame. Social workers were experiencing increasing pressure and stress, and there was a national shortage of social workers as a result of people leaving the profession and a failure to recruit new members of staff. The Scottish Executive commissioned a review of social work in 2004. The review group was asked to take a fundamental look at all aspects of social work and make recommendations on how services should be developed. The report of the review group, *Changing Lives: Report of the 21st Century Social Work Review* was published in 2006.

The review group recognised that 'more of the same' simply was not an option. It suggested that:

> Increasing demand, greater complexity and rising expectations mean that the current situation is not sustainable. Tomorrow's solutions will need to engage people as active participants, delivering accessible, responsive services of the highest quality and promoting wellbeing. (Scottish Executive, 2006d, p. 8)

The review presented a clear message that the nature of social work was changing. It argued that social workers have a distinctive set of skills, values and knowledge that must be used in a more flexible way in order to support and empower people to take responsibility for their own lives.

The key feature of the new social work is the emphasis on personalisation – a key theme reflected throughout this book. Services must be tailored to meet individual needs in a flexible way that will support and empower people to achieve their own goals and aspirations. The traditional model whereby people were expected to fit in with existing, inflexible services regardless of need, want or ability is no longer acceptable. In order to do this successfully, the report argued, social workers must work more effectively with individuals, families and communities and work in new ways with other agencies.

In Scotland, the partnership agenda is characterised by its focus on service users and personalised services to ensure services are organised around the needs of individuals rather than service providers. There is commitment to driving up quality, encouraging innovation and creativity, building in continuous improvement, and improving efficiency and productivity. The key is to join up services and minimise separation, sharing best practice across organisations. In line with the recommendations of the 21st Century Review (Scottish Executive, 2006d), there has been a move to strengthen accountability by moving power and resources to the front line, strengthening local responsibility and accountability (Hudson, 2007). Hudson (2007) points out that a similar commitment to partnership working exists in England. The picture in England is more complicated, however, as other policy objectives such as a commitment to the market model compete with the partnership agenda (see also Cook *et al.*, 2007 for a more detailed discussion of partnership working).

The 21st Century Review raised concerns around the ways in which the demands on social workers resulted in professional roles becoming focused on managing access to existing services, rather than on helping people to find solutions to their problems. As a result people had become passive recipients of services rather than active participants. In order to overcome this, it was recommended that social workers should:

- respect the right to self-determination;
- promote participation;
- take a whole-person approach;
- understand each individual in the context of family and community;
- identify and build on strengths.

The key challenge for social workers is to adopt a new role which involves providing services which people find easy to use and which are better equipped to help them find their own solutions. In order to enable the service user to take control of their own care a range of service initiatives have been developed. These include direct payments and individual budgets, In Control and personalised and self-directed care.

Direct payments

Direct payments were introduced in Scotland, England and Wales in 1997 as a result of the Community Care (Direct Payments) Act 1996. Originally, local authorities were able to make cash payments to service users under the age of 65 with physical or sensory impairments, learning disabilities or mental health problems. This was later extended to include people over the age of 65, 16- and 17-year-olds, and parents of disabled children (Pearson, 2006). Progress on direct payments has been slow and the uptake by different service user groups has been disappointing. This is despite changes in legislation in Scotland, set out in the 2002 Community Care and Health (Scotland) Act which placed a mandatory duty on local authorities to offer direct payments to those service users who were eligible. The latest figures published by the Scottish Executive (2007c) showed take-up of direct payments by service user group and local authority. A total of 1829 direct payments were made in 2006. This was a substantial increase from 912 in 2004 and from 207 in 2001. Fife had the highest take-up rate across all service user groups, with 262 people receiving direct payments in 2006. Despite being the largest local authority in Scotland, Glasgow City made only the fourth highest number of direct payments, with 124 people receiving them in 2006. In terms of service user group, take-up continued to be highest among people with physical disabilities. In 2006, 950 people with a physical disability received a direct payment, while 424 payments were made to people with a learning disability and 62 payments were made to people with a mental health problem (Scottish Executive, 2007c). The use of direct payments can bring many positive benefits (see, for example, Pearson, 2006; Riddell *et al.*, 2006), including greater independence and control. It can also be cost-effective, as work by Heywood and Turner (2007) has shown.

According to Pearson (2006), there are several reasons why take-up of direct payments has continued to be lower than might be expected. In particular, in Scotland, although personalisation has featured on a number of policy agendas, this has not been linked to an independent living agenda, as has been the case in England (Pearson, 2006). There has been a lack of cohesion about the direct payment agenda across a number of Scottish government departments. A Scottish Executive working group on Direct Payments for Older People also identified a number of contributing factors to low uptake. These included a lack of awareness about direct payments and self-directed support among service users, and the need to 'win over' staff at all levels by introducing a lead officer in each local authority (Scottish Executive, 2007b). The allocation of £1.8 million in 2005 and £2 million the following year to develop support organisations and designated direct payment posts in areas where developments have been particularly slow does, however, demonstrate the overall commitment of the Scottish government to this agenda.

The key issue for the social worker is to understand what his or her role is in relation to the direct payment process. The role of the care manager in this process would be to work in partnership with an individual to find out what support they need and what it is possible to provide. The individual then undergoes an assessment process, including a self-assessment, and at the end of this process a personal care plan is agreed between the individual and the care manager. The individual will then receive an individual budget to pay for their support needs. Research has suggested that direct payments have been the subject of misunderstanding and stereotyping, and that an assumption is made that service users generally, and particularly those with learning disabilities or mental health problems, are not capable of managing the process. According to Williams and Holman (2006), people with learning disabilities were included in the planning process for direct payments at a relatively late stage after previous attempts to exclude them. This resulted in a lack of suitable support schemes and structures being available for this group (Williams and Holman, 2006). Practitioners may find it harder to accept direct payments as an appropriate method for people with learning disabilities if adequate support mechanisms are not obviously in place (Williams, 2006).

People with learning disabilities face a number of particular barriers when it comes to accessing direct payments. These include a lack of accessible information alongside the range of negative attitudes outlined above, which assume people with learning disabilities cannot manage the process. There are also concerns about the quality of care that people might receive as a result of direct payments, as it may be more difficult to monitor and manage quality assurance processes and procedures. Pearson (2006) has suggested that there is a need for a cultural change incorporating a shift in values and attitudes if self-directed support and user choice and control are to become a reality (Pearson, 2006). This is echoed in the 21st Century Review recommendations outlined above. People with learning disabilities are likely to require intensive and ongoing support in order to make direct payments work for them. A number of the recommendations made as a result of research on direct payments generally (see Hasler and Stewart, 2004) have particular salience for people with learning disabilities. These might include appointing a direct payments champion for people with learning disabilities, reducing the bureaucracy demanded of the direct payment user, providing staff training on values, led by people with learning disabilities, and introducing variable rates of pay for personal assistants so that those supporting people with more complex needs are paid more (see also Davey *et al.*, 2007).

Self-directed support

The Scottish Executive published new national guidance on self-directed support in July 2007 (Scottish Executive, 2007b). The guidance was issued under the Social Work (Scotland) Act 1968 and replaced earlier guidance on direct payments issued in June 2003. The aim of the guidance was to improve take-up of self-directed support and it was based on best practice recommendations from national working groups, national research work and the evidence of the Care Inquiry (Scottish Executive, 2007b). The guidance has defined self-directed support as:

> part of the whole range of practical solutions to disabled or older people's meaningful integration into mainstream society. It includes services for children, for those using mental health services and for older people in receipt of free personal care. The flexibility achieved is such that those with complex needs can also have self-directed support using the Adults with Incapacity (Scotland) Act 2000 to safeguard their interests ... self-directed support is part of Shifting the Balance of Scotland's health care towards sustaining and improving health and preventing longer term conditions through an emphasis on self-help and support that is continuous, integrated and individualised .... (Scottish Executive, 2007b, p. 2)

The terms self-directed support and direct payments are often used interchangeably. The more recent use of the term self-directed support subtly shifts the emphasis from the method of delivery (i.e. direct payments) to the outcome for individuals. The emphasis is on organising social care in a way which enables people to take control of their lives and fulfil their role as citizens (again a key theme of this book). The guidance identified a number of specific tasks for local authorities to fund. These included:

- a local support service which, where possible, should be independent and user-led;
- early involvement of individuals with the local support service to assist with self-assessment and care planning;
- other essential training for individuals on self-directed support, and training of personal assistants (PAs);
- all basic costs within a PA employers package where appropriate;
- designated self-directed support lead officers or teams within each local authority;
- training on self-directed support for care managers, finance managers and local authority directors;

- enhanced disclosures for PAs employed by individuals on self-directed support.

According to the latest research into the process of implementing direct payments (Pearson, 2006; Williams and Holman, 2006; Davey *et al.*, 2007), the barriers are relatively straightforward to overcome if adequate resources are dedicated to the above tasks outlined by the Scottish Executive (see also Rummery, 2006). What might be more difficult to change are the attitudes and values of key staff members and service providers.

In Control

People with learning disabilities might need additional support in order to access direct payments or self-directed care. This is the purpose of the In Control project which is a new way of helping people with learning disabilities achieve self-directed support. In Control takes a person-centred approach and assists people and their families to work in partnership with local authorities and other agencies in developing and controlling services. The In Control approach is underpinned by a number of key ethical principles and values. These include a belief in the right to independent living, the right to an individual budget and the right to self-determination. In Control was established in England in 2003 and is currently being piloted in four local authority areas in Scotland. The Scottish Consortium for Learning Disabilities and ALTRUM are responsible for developing In Control in Scotland. It would appear that the use of initiatives such as In Control, alongside the greater use of direct payments, individual budgets and self-directed care, offer people with learning disabilities the opportunity to become valued citizens.

According to Duffy (2003) there are six goals that people with learning disabilities must achieve in order to become active and valued citizens. These are self-determination, direction, money, a home of one's own, adequate support where this is required, and community living. He suggests that these are the key elements of citizenship. Although the initiatives outlined in the chapter until this point can certainly assist, a note of caution and realism is required. For many people with learning disabilities to become full and active citizens, a significant amount of work is still required – not least in changing the attitudes of policy makers, service providers and the wider community. The challenge for social workers and other service providers is to adapt and reconcile their own roles for this new way of working. Social workers and other professionals are increasingly likely to be viewed as enablers rather than providers of services.

Changing expectations in relation to day opportunities

Sitting alongside this changing role for social workers, which involves enabling and empowering people with learning disabilities to make decisions and take control of their own lives, is a change in the traditional notion of day opportunities for people with learning disabilities. The reconfiguration of traditional social work day services accords with the trend towards the mainstreaming of services. *The Same As You*? stated that the role of day centres should change. It argued that no one should go to a day centre full time but that people should have alternative day opportunities for at least part of the week. As part of the review (Scottish Executive, 2000a), a short-life working group was formed to look at day opportunities for people with learning disabilities. The report of the working group – *Make My Day! The Same As You? National Implementation Group: Report of the Day Services Sub Group* – was published in 2006 (Scottish Executive, 2006a) and is discussed briefly in Chapter 1.

The How's It Going? survey of what matters most to people with learning disabilities in Scotland (Curtice, 2006) suggests that having friends and being able to go out more is of crucial importance. People with learning disabilities want to be able to access facilities within their communities, including shops, sports, leisure centres and restaurants (Curtice, 2006). Providing community-based opportunities is therefore vital. The latest statistical release from the Scottish Executive on the implementation of *The Same As You*? showed that around 6,689 adults with learning disabilities in Scotland attended a day centre in a typical week, representing 29% of all adults with learning disabilities in Scotland. The numbers of adults attending day centres had fallen for the third year running, from 41% (7,433 adults) in 2003 to 29% in 2006. Of those people attending a day centre in 2006, only 26% attended full time. This had fallen from 27% in 2005 and from 36% in 2003. There were 3,035 people who did not attend day centres but received alternative day opportunities. This figure has remained fairly constant since 2005 but has undergone a 54% increase since 2003 (Scottish Executive, 2007a).

The picture varies by local authority. In East Ayrshire, for example, 60% of all adults attending a day centre did so five days a week. This compares to three authorities where no one attending a day centre did so five days a week (Scottish Executive, 2007a). In Glasgow, there has been a move away from centre-based services towards locality-based services, with a focus on providing more opportunities within the community (Glasgow City Council, 2000). In Glasgow, there were three main aims in relation to younger people with learning disabilities – to make more use of further education, to look at employment opportunities, and to make greater use of mainstream leisure opportunities. This is a trend that has been reflected in other local authority areas across Scotland. This would seem to be a positive development, and social work departments would argue that traditional day centre settings are not always the best option for young people leaving school.

However, the author's own research suggests that alternatives have not always focused on further education, training and employment. In one local authority, for example, a school leavers group was run 'in the spirit of not assuming they [young people with learning disabilities] would automatically leave school and go to the day centre'. Young people met outwith the day centre and did a range of activities. These were mainly leisure activities and there was no focus on employment or training. Additionally, there was no exit plan for young people to leave the group and so it would appear that it took on the day centre role in a different setting. Although this was a genuine attempt to move away from the traditional day centre model, it did not offer an imaginative or flexible alternative that might have assisted young people to move on to further education, training or employment.

Although the statistics presented here paint a positive picture, the move away from the traditional day centre model does not appear to have been welcomed by everyone. For a lot of parents in particular, the traditional day centre approach provided a respite function. This discussion also raises the crucial issue that some people with learning disabilities may perhaps need a long-term alternative to employment and training. It is likely that these difficulties will be exacerbated for those people with more severe disabilities. For these people, the movement away from the traditional day centre is perhaps unhelpful.

These issues have interesting parallels with the literature on the closure of long-stay hospitals in Britain (see, for example, Cattermole *et al.*, 1990; Stalker and Hunter, 1999; Forrester-Jones *et al.*, 2002; Whoriskey, 2003). These studies have suggested that people with learning disabilities returning to the community are likely to enjoy some benefits to their quality of life, although social inclusion is by no means guaranteed. Initially, the closure of long-stay hospitals focused on a rehabilitation model with a series of progressions. Independent living was the end goal. More recently it has been accepted that this model is not suitable for everyone. Some people will require lifelong support (see, for example, Petch *et al.*, 2000). The evidence presented here would suggest that the same is true in relation to day opportunities. It would appear, then, that the most important thing is to provide both choice and flexibility coupled with an acknowledgement that long-term support may be a necessity. Services need to be flexible enough to provide a balanced approach: mainstream services where appropriate, with specialist provision for those whose needs make it essential or for those who prefer it. This does have resource implications, but these need to be worked through if the principles of inclusion are to be embraced.

Local area co-ordination

The review of learning disability services (Scottish Executive, 2000a) also recommended the introduction of local area co-ordinators whose role would be to co-ordinate services and provide information, deliver support for families and organise funding. Local area co-ordination originated in Australia: it is driven by the needs of people and is designed around each person (again reflecting the philosophy outlined above). *The Same As You*? (Scottish Executive, 2000a) suggested that local area co-ordinators could have a range of professional backgrounds. Each would be responsible for supporting around 50 people so that they would know them personally and be able to respond to individual needs. It was envisaged that local area co-ordinators would help people make plans for the future and assist them to navigate their way around the services that were available within their local community. A key aspect of the role was to enable people with learning disabilities to build networks and make friendships within their local community. It was thought that local area co-ordinators would have a budget which would be used to provide funding directly to people who use services (Scottish Executive, 2000a, p. 20).

Overall, the review recommended that the role of local area co-ordinators should be to help people with learning disabilities to lead full lives. Achieving this would require better assessment of people's social and health care needs. This was to include an assessment of an individual's wants, their strengths, skills and needs and what they require to achieve their goals (Scottish Executive, 2000a). The local area co-ordinator would also be responsible for producing a personal life plan for every adult with learning disabilities (who wanted one). These plans would aid long-term planning and would replace community care assessments. The plan would describe how the person with learning disabilities, their family and professionals would work together to help the person lead a fuller life. The personal life plan is a process for continual listening and learning and it is based primarily on the views of the individual (where possible) alongside the views of their family, friends and professionals who work with them. It should act upon what is important to someone now and in the future. (Scottish Executive, 2000a).

Such was the importance given to local area co-ordination that a short-life working group was established. It published its recommendations in August 2002 (Scottish Executive, 2002). It found that local area co-ordination was being implemented in different ways in different areas, and was sometimes not following some of the essential principles of the model. The group argued that, if used appropriately, local area co-ordination could reduce inappropriate dependence on formal services by supporting the practice of self-directed care and developing and funding alternative community supports. At the time of publication, it was not clear how the role of the local area co-ordinator would relate to that of the care manager. Local area co-ordination was thought to differ from care management in various ways: it makes support available throughout life (i.e. for children as well as adults); it emphasises the development of strengths and capacities rather than the need for services; and its main purpose is to develop informal and community supports for individuals (Scottish Executive, 2002). It was hoped that local area co-ordination might mean that some people with learning disabilities may not have to move into the care management system because local area co-ordination should have built up a network of community-based supports (Scottish Executive, 2002). Again, this raises issues around role clarity and purpose. At a time of changing services and philosophies it is essential that key staff are clear as to their roles and responsibilities. The short-life working group recommended that the Scottish Executive should issue guidance on local area co-ordination based on the outcomes and principles developed by the working group.

A recent Scottish Executive statistical release shows progress made to date in each of these areas. In 2006, a local area co-ordination service was provided by 28 (of 32) local authorities in Scotland. This had risen from 14 in 2003 (Scottish Executive, 2007a). Around 2,295 adults had benefited from the services of a local area co-ordinator. This equates to approximately 10% of all adults with learning disabilities known across Scotland. An estimated 82% of adults using the services of a local area co-ordinator were aged between 21 and 64. The proportion of adults in receipt of the service varied from 1% in two local authorities to 44% in Argyll and Bute and 50% in Moray. In addition, 29% of adults known to local authorities had a personal life plan or person-centred plan (Scottish Executive, 2007a). There had been a large increase in the number of personal life plans, from 5,662 in 2005 to 6,723 in 2006. This can be explained in part by improved data collection methods. The number of life plans varied by local authority. East Dunbartonshire performed well: 71% of adults with learning disabilities known to the council had a plan (Scottish Executive, 2007a). None of the young people with learning disabilities in the author's own research project had a personal life plan, nor had they received the services of a local area co-ordinator.

Evaluating the implementation of local area co-ordination in Scotland

Very little research into the implementation or effectiveness of local area co-ordination has been conducted. A recent study by Stalker and colleagues brought together the evidence that was available in a comprehensive report (Stalker *et al.*, 2007). As well as conducting a literature review, they asked local area co-ordinators to complete a pro forma, and carried out interviews with 35 local area co-ordinators and with managers. Case studies of local area co-ordination in practice were also conducted. The researchers found that clearly identified, measurable outcomes were difficult to extract from the process. From the interviews with local area co-ordinators, however, three main areas of achievement were identified. These were a better overall quality of life (a notoriously difficult concept to measure), specific differences to individuals' lives, and particular areas of work such as the transition to adulthood. The benefits of local area co-ordination identified included having time to build relationships with individuals and families, enabling people to identify their own needs and work towards meeting these, and building links with their local communities via a variety of networks (Stalker *et al.*, 2007). Individuals and their families highly valued the work of local area co-ordinators and felt they had made an important contribution to their lives.

As mentioned above, Stalker *et al.* (2007) also found wide variation in the implementation of local area co-ordination. At the time of their research there were 59 local area co-ordinators in post, employed mostly by local authorities. The scale of the task varied considerably by area, although most local area co-ordinators worked with both children and adults with learning disabilities. In only 11 areas did local area co-ordinators have access to dedicated budgets, mostly amounting to less than £5,000 (Stalker *et al.*, 2007). The experience of local area co-ordinators once in post varied by the area in which they were based. For example, not all local area co-ordinators received an induction upon commencement of their post, and the type and amount of training offered varied. Most local area co-ordinators said they would value further training on community capacity building and the creation of neighbourhood (defined as local and community resources to provide natural supports for families) – a key feature of the job.

The research found considerable variation in the number of people supported by local area co-ordinators. This ranged from one to 42 individuals. In addition, very little time was spent on community capacity building. This was thought to stem not only from a lack of time but also from disinterest, and at times resistance, from some local communities. Local area co-ordination was found to have a number of distinctive features. In particular, its commitment to a person-centred value base and its perceived lack of bureaucracy were thought to be positive features. In addition, local area co-ordinators were thought to be better placed to carry out preventative work and to challenge existing disadvantage or discrimination while at the same time promoting inclusion (Stalker *et al.*, 2007, p. 4).

Although the local area co-ordinators interviewed as part of the research mainly embraced the values outlined above, a small number felt these were idealistic or even unrealistic. In addition to this, some reported continuing confusion or tension between the role of the local area co-ordinator and the role of the social worker or care manager. In order for the relationship to work well, there was a requirement for both parties to accept that the relationship and the associated activities of each role were complementary. Difficulties arose in at least three local authority areas where local area co-ordinators were expected to take on a care management role.

The research by Stalker and colleagues suggested that overall, around half of the local area co-ordinators felt well supported by senior staff within their organisation. Worryingly, however, in nine authorities, local area co-ordinators reported feeling isolated and devalued. Five local area co-ordinators also felt undermined in their role (Stalker *et al.*, 2007).

At the time of Stalker's research, seven local authorities had yet to appoint local area co-ordinators. The majority of these had specific hopes or plans to implement local area co-ordination in the near future. Others felt it was possible to implement the recommendations of *The Same As You?* (Scottish Executive, 2000a) without necessarily creating posts with that title. They gave examples of the expansion or development of existing services to show how they were working to achieve the recommendations (Stalker *et al.*, 2007). Barriers to the implementation of local area co-ordination appeared to be practical rather than ideological. In particular, budgetary constraints and embedded bureaucratic structures were identified as key concerns.

Discussion

The evaluation conducted by Stalker and her colleagues (2007), which has been discussed in some depth here, concluded by suggesting that there was a need for national debate around how certain aspects of the local area co-ordination ethos relate to the structural and political context of Scotland as opposed to Australia. In particular, it recognised the need to develop local area co-ordination without an equivalent reduction in social work and health services for those who need them. Caution and realism were also required in providing appropriate family support and building community capacity.

Local area co-ordination seems to present an excellent opportunity to provide – perhaps for the first time – truly person-centred services for people with learning disabilities and their families. Those involved – people with learning disabilities, their families and local area co-ordinators themselves – highly value the service, and there has been evidence of positive outcomes including increased independence, choice and inclusion. However, implementation of the service has been patchy across the country and people with learning disabilities are not currently receiving an equitable service.

Overall, this chapter has highlighted a key trend in service provision for people with learning disabilities. A significant shift, both in policy rhetoric and within practice, changed the focus from the provision of relatively rigid, inflexible services towards handing control (and money) to people with learning disabilities and their families. The developments outlined in this chapter should result in greater social inclusion. People will, in theory, have greater control over the services they receive and will become more fully involved in the decision-making process, thus becoming more active and valued citizens. Such developments must be viewed in a positive light. Challenges do, however, remain, none more so than the continued slow implementation of each of the developments. In addition, there is concern that service providers do not agree what social inclusion and citizenship for people with learning disabilities actually means, and what the best methods are for promoting it.

For such developments to succeed there is a need to ensure several things in two key areas. Firstly, people with learning disabilities should have the support they need to access services and make decisions. There must also be a recognition that families may not always be best placed to provide this support. Secondly, social work staff and service providers should be aware of what their role is in this new policy landscape. Current frontline staff will require training, and education providers will need to adapt their curriculum in recognition of these changes. There is a need to challenge those attitudes which suggest that people with learning disabilities are not capable of taking control of the services they receive.

These developments raise questions which are not easy to address but which the reader must be aware of. Firstly, what does the future hold for those service users who do not necessarily wish to take control of the services they receive, or to take responsibility for holding their own budget? Secondly, is moving towards increasingly individualised services the route to social inclusion by empowering people to access local, community-based services, or will those people responsible for holding their own budget find themselves increasingly isolated? Further research is required to address these questions.

Chapter 6

Conclusions

During the course of this book it has been possible to identify a number of key trends and changes in policy for people with learning disabilities in Scotland and across the UK as a whole. Although the focus of this book has been on Scottish policy, relevant areas of similarity to, or difference from, the rest of the UK have been highlighted where appropriate. Throughout the book, a number of questions have been raised – the main one being the extent to which policy changes have resulted in greater social inclusion for people with learning disabilities. It has been possible to identify a number of ways in which people with learning disabilities have enjoyed greater opportunities. The book has also identified the types of support people with learning disabilities require to make the most of these opportunities.

Key trends in education

Within the education system, there have been increasing moves towards inclusion, accompanied by changing definitions of the target group. There has been a move away from the traditional notion of special educational needs towards a much broader definition of additional support needs, which better reflects today's society and recognises the common issues and barriers that children and young people with a range of support needs face. Broadening the client group to such an extent is likely to have financial implications, and there is likely to be a much wider group of young people competing for scare resources. This may result in services being prioritised for particular groups of young people.

Young people with learning disabilities leaving school are more likely to be educated within a mainstream setting. Those who are not are still able to access a greater number of opportunities upon leaving school. However, young people with learning disabilities leaving school today face similar difficulties to young people in the general population. The collapse of the youth labour market and the recession of the early 1990s have meant that the type of work traditionally done by young people is no longer readily available. In addition, globalisation has changed the nature of employment (see Jolly, 2000; Roulstone, 2002). Disabled workers are entering an increasingly risky employment domain, where more and more of the work available is short-term and part-time, with a growth in self-employment.

Although the growing flexibility of the labour market might bring some advantages to disabled workers in terms of ability to adapt working hours and so on, it is likely to result in employees having to satisfy increasingly stringent criteria to retain employment (Jolly, 2000).

Declining employment opportunities for young people generally have occurred at a time when there is a growing expectation of participation in the labour market for people with disabilities. As a result of this changing rhetoric, young adults with disabilities are no longer expected to leave school for a life in an adult training centre. Instead, they are expected to enjoy the opportunities of further education, training and employment available to all young people. However, disabled young people are less likely to sustain paid employment (Hirst and Baldwin, 1994), live independently (Pascall and Hendey, 2002) or marry and have children (May and Simpson, 2003). In relation to further education, training and employment, they face a range of barriers that relate to their status as a disabled person. The author's own research suggests that young disabled people continue to experience segregation within further education (regardless of whether they attended a mainstream or special school). Furthermore, negative attitudes, low expectations and a lack of appropriate support services can mean that employment is not even considered a viable option in every case. Young disabled people who do continue to aspire to find employment face barriers in the form of a lack of suitable employment opportunities, a lack of qualifications and the inflexibility of the benefits system. Indeed, despite the increased choice of routes post-school and access to support services, young people with learning disabilities are more likely than young people in the general population to be part of the NEET group (not in education, employment or training).

According to Bignall *et al.* (2000), although there has been a great deal of rhetoric about opening up choices to young disabled people, in practice the structures of education and training channel them down particular routes which may not reflect their own aspirations. Bignall *et al.* (2000) argue that for young disabled people choice is very structured. This reflects a key debate within recent sociological writings on youth transitions, namely whether young people are free agents able to exercise choice and agency, or whether they are constrained by a range of structural factors.

Key trends in the fields of training and employment

Changing attitudes have resulted in a greater expectation that people with learning disabilities will move into the world of training and employment. The book has highlighted the range of support services and training programmes that are available to assist people into the labour market. The sheer number of training providers and programmes that are available reflects the priority which government places on this area in the UK and Scotland. Research has shown that people with learning disabilities aspire to find paid employment (although other areas of their lives, such as having a home of their own or being able to see their friends, may have greater priority) (Curtice, 2006). The drive towards employment should certainly assist people with learning disabilities to achieve greater social inclusion, and the broader spectrum of training and employment opportunities available is a positive development. This shift in policy direction does, however, raise a number of issues.

A recurring question is whether services should focus on those people closest to the labour market. Funding mechanisms and targets placed on services by governing bodies have made this an almost inevitable outcome. In addition, the growing focus on supply-side measures means that those people who find it easiest to adapt and fit in to the current labour market are more likely to enjoy successful outcomes. Services such as New Deal for Disabled People and Work Preparation may find their structures make them less able to deal with those people who need more support. Supply-side measures echo the principle of normalisation and its claims that disabled people should attempt to fit in to society as much as possible. The emphasis is on change within the individual; in this case they must acquire work-related skills and undergo lengthy periods of training to increase their employability. Much less attention is paid to tackling barriers to employment, such as the attitudes of employers or the inflexibility of the benefits system, as may be advocated by the social model of disability.

To this end there has been a growing recognition, initially among disability writers and increasingly among policy makers, that supply-side measures alone will be ineffective for many disabled people. In order to facilitate greater inclusion within the workplace for people with disabilities, training programmes and employment services must be accompanied by a reformed, more flexible benefits system which sees the transition from benefits to employment as a continuum, alongside more effective anti-discrimination legislation. The UK government has pledged to move people off Incapacity Benefit into employment and increasingly the focus is on encouraging disabled people into employment. As yet, this commitment has not been given the financial backing required to be successful, and expenditure on disability programmes falls short of spending on other groups such as lone parents and young people. In addition, despite the rhetoric, some policies continue to appear to be influenced to some extent by a medical definition of disability where the focus is on individual impairment rather than on societal barriers to employment. The UK government continues to emphasise the link between rights and obligations, and debates around citizenship often point to employment as a defining feature.

The author's own research showed that people with learning disabilities face a number of barriers in finding and keeping paid employment. Yet despite this, policy makers continue to regard employment as the principal marker of adult status and citizenship. Literature on employability and supported employment suggests that, although employment brings with it some very clear benefits to adults in the general population as well as to those with a range of disabilities, it can also bring with it features which might have a negative impact on mental health. Supported employment is regarded as a panacea and is thought to be the most appropriate way of encouraging labour market participation for people with learning (and other) disabilities. Policy makers appear undeterred by research findings that question some aspects of the supported employment model in the British context, particularly in relation to financial gain and social interaction. In addition, it would appear that little consideration has been given to alternatives for those young people and adults who find the goal of employment difficult to achieve.

Who should be responsible for the provision of ongoing support?

This book has highlighted the extent to which people with learning disabilities require ongoing support in order to participate fully in society. Current training and employment services such as Get Ready for Work, Training for Work, Work Step and Supported Employment are all time-limited. In the majority of cases, funding for these services relies on staff meeting certain pre-defined targets. This usually involves moving a certain number of clients on to a 'positive outcome' such as a paid job, a supported employment place, a training programme or a college place. This can put pressure on staff to move clients on before they are ready and without the adequate support measures being put in place. This raises the dilemma of who should be responsible for providing ongoing support. The hope is that natural support mechanisms can be developed within the work-place (indeed this is one of the key principles of the supported employment model – see, for example, Schneider, 1998a; O'Bryan *et al.*, 2000; Wilson, 2003). However, these natural support mechanisms are not always forthcoming. The associated financial implications mean this dilemma is unlikely to be an easy one to resolve.

Similar dilemmas exist in relation to meeting the health needs of people with learning disabilities. Chapter 4 highlighted the debates that exist in relation to who should be meeting the health care needs of this group. Since the hospital closure programme took effect across the UK, this question has become particularly salient, because prior to this people's health needs were likely to be met (not necessarily effectively) by learning disability specialists within hospitals. As increasing numbers of people with learning disabilities have moved into their local communities, there has been an increased expectation that health needs should be met by primary care practitioners such as the GP and practice nurse. While this move towards mainstreaming should be regarded as a positive development, the introduction of health checks for people with learning disabilities has revealed a high level of unmet health needs among this group. This suggests that primary care teams are not working effectively with people with learning disabilities. By reviewing existing research in this area, this book has identified a need for better training for primary care professionals in a bid to not only improve practice but change attitudes.

How can people with learning disabilities become valued citizens?

Clearly the support mechanisms currently available in relation to health, education and employment are not always adequate, and there is a need for more flexible, ongoing support for disabled people as discussed above. People with learning disabilities are unlikely to achieve social inclusion or become full and active citizens unless appropriate (i.e. flexible and ongoing) support mechanisms are put in place. Service providers need to question the objectives, goals and roles of their services. Is an intervention worthwhile if it assists a person with learning disabilities into an employment situation where they are likely to continue to be marginalised, both financially and socially? A more meaningful intervention might offer people with learning disabilities support to make choices and empower them to act upon these choices. Similarly, although traditional day centres are no longer regarded as an appropriate post-school option for the majority of young people with learning disabilities, evidence exists that shows people being marginalised within mainstream college and employment settings (see Chapters 2 and 3). Ultimately value must be given to the range of activities and options available to people with learning disabilities, rather than promoting unrealistic or unattainable goals.

Proponents of the social model of disability in its most extreme form would argue that disability would not exist if it were not for the structural barriers created by society. This view has influenced a range of policy developments which, in relation to employment for example, suggest that anyone can get a job if adequate support is available. The experiences of some disabled people suggest that this is not always the case. This has created a legacy of unrealistic expectations. Traditional theories of citizenship and social justice have exacerbated the pressure to aspire to paid employment by undervaluing alternative roles and ways of participating in society. They reinforce the view that those people who are unable to sustain paid employment (or training and further education), even with support, have failed and should be less valued than others in society. What is needed is a concept that values the different roles and activities undertaken by disabled people within society. Writers from the disability studies tradition (see Sapey, 2000; Williams, 2001; Harris, 2002; Watson *et al.*, 2004) have drawn on feminist theories of citizenship to call for renewed concepts of independence and interdependence. Independence should not only be understood as the ability to sustain a place at college or on a training course or the ability to hold down a paid job. Instead independence should be about having the support to make choices about one's own life and to pursue these choices without encountering disabling barriers.

Passing control to people with learning disabilities

The recent changes within the field of social work and related services appear to reflect these concerns. As outlined in Chapter 5, there have been a range of policy measures within the field of community care which aim to create increasingly person-centred, flexible and empowering services for people with learning disabilities and other service groups. These innovations include the introduction of local area co-ordinators, as well as the move towards individualised budgets and self-directed care. It is possible to identify a number of key trends.

Increasingly, there has been a shifting emphasis towards joint working and partnership working. The joint working agenda is not new. In Scotland, attempts have been made to increase joint working since the inception of the Joint Future Agenda in 2003 (Stewart *et al.*, 2003). A more recent development, however, is the drive towards partnership working with service users and their families. This can be witnessed, for instance, in the increased emphasis on service user and carer involvement in a number of areas —policy making, service provision and management, education and training, and so on. There has been a movement away from the notion of service users having to fit in with existing services towards a philosophy of personalisation where individual service users and their families exercise choice and control in order to access services that meet their needs. Social workers and other professionals should no longer view their role as only being about the provision of services. Instead, they should be empowering people with learning disabilities to take control of their own lives. This is exemplified well by the In Control scheme discussed in Chapter 5. In theory, service users and their families should have greater choice and control, and this should assist in promoting social inclusion. In practice, it is yet to be seen whether this change in philosophy will have an impact on social inclusion and participation in the community. Professionals face challenging times in adapting to their new role. For people with learning disabilities, however, it would appear that there is some scope for optimism. Indeed, *How's It Going?* (Curtice, 2006) – reporting on the largest survey of people with learning disabilities in Scotland – suggested that since the publication of *The Same As You*? in 2000, 66% of those who responded felt their lives had got better compared with only 34% who thought their lives had got worse. For 27%, things had stayed the same. Those who felt their lives had got better attributed this to having a new home, more freedom and more friends. For those who felt that things had got worse, the main problem was thought to be a reduction in support (Curtice, 2006).

Direct payments and self-directed care might be regarded as a key mechanism to enable people with learning disabilities to participate within their communities as active citizens. Rummery (2006) builds a powerful argument to suggest that direct payments should enable disabled people to be treated as full citizens:

> In campaigning for direct payments, disabled people are campaigning for the right to undertake their citizenship duties – not only to 'share in the full social heritage and to live the civilised life according to the standards prevailing in society' but also to 'live the life of a good citizen, giving such services as can promote the welfare of the community'. (p. 647)

Likewise, individualised budgets (in England and Wales) and personalised budgets (in Scotland) have been particularly significant for people with learning disabilities. In a similar way to direct payments, these new budgets offer service users the freedom, choice and control to tailor-make packages of support best suited to their needs. Again, this may assist in shifting perceptions of disabled people as passive recipients of care, giving them the right to be treated as equal citizens.

Discussion

People with learning disabilities are experiencing an increasing range of options in relation to education, training, employment, leisure opportunities and health care, and hence it can be argued that they experience greater social inclusion than previously. They remain, however, in a marginalised position, similar to that of other groups of disadvantaged people. They are more likely, for example, to be over-represented in the group of young people who are not in education, employment or training. In addition, those who do manage to attain employment find it does not necessarily lead to greater social inclusion. The type of job occupied by a person with a learning disability is likely to be routine, manual work with poor pay and little chance of progression or promotion. Likewise, for those in further education there is little opportunity to progress from a specialist course to a mainstream one. In addition, research has found evidence of only superficial social contact with peers within the workplace or college setting. In order to maintain or achieve social inclusion, people with learning disabilities require support that is flexible, tailored to the needs of the individual and ongoing. Who should provide this support is a difficult question to answer. However, the experiences of people using existing services such as Get Ready for Work and the Beattie key worker service suggest that these have not always been successful in helping people attain the sustainability that has proved so illusive.

It might be argued that even low-paid, mundane work is better than no employment at all, and it is reasonable to assume that someone who is economically inactive and in receipt of benefits cannot be socially included. Much depends, however, on how social inclusion and its opposite, social exclusion, are viewed. If the caring, parenting, civic, social and political activities that disabled people (and other disadvantaged groups) undertake are equally valued alongside paid employment, then people with learning disabilities have undoubtedly made progress towards achieving social inclusion and citizenship status. With the shift of control to people with learning disabilities via mechanisms such as direct payments, self-directed care and local area co-ordination, things are moving in the right direction. This should not allow for complacency, however. In order to continue to empower people with learning disabilities to achieve their goals, the government (at both a Scottish and UK level) will have to make a continued commitment in the form of resources for appropriate support. Promoting social inclusion for people with learning disabilities, as has been suggested throughout this book, is the responsibility not only of the individual but of all those involved in their lives, including family members, practitioners and policy makers within mainstream and specialist settings, at local and national levels.

References

Adams, E. and Smart, D. (2005) *Mapping Employability and Support Services for Disengaged Young People*, Edinburgh: Blackwell Publishing

Barnes, C. (1990) *Cabbage Syndrome: The Social Construction of Dependence*, London: Falmer Press

Barnes, C. (2003) 'Work is a four letter word? Disability, work and welfare', paper to the Working Futures: Disability and Work Seminar, University of Sunderland, 3 December 2003

Barnes, C. and Mercer, G. (1996) *Exploring the Divide: Illness and Disability*, Leeds: Disability Press

Barnes, C., Mercer, G. and Shakespeare, T. (1999) *Exploring Disability: A Sociological Introduction*, Cambridge: The Policy Press

Barr, O., Gilgunn, J., Kane, T. and Moore, G. (1999) 'Health screening for people with learning disabilities by a community learning disability nursing service in Northern Ireland', *Journal of Advanced Nursing*, Vol. 29, No. 6, pp. 1482–91

Bass, M. and Drewett, R. (1997) *Real Work: Supported Employment for People with Learning Disabilities*, Sheffield: Joint Unit for Social Services Research

Bauman, Z. (1988) *Freedom*, Milton Keynes: Open University Press

Beange, H., McElduff, A. and Baker, W. (1995) 'Medical disorders of adults with mental retardation: a population study', *American Journal of Mental Retardation*, Vol. 99, No. 6, pp. 595–604

Beyer, S. and Kilsby, M. (1996a) 'Supported employment in Britain', *Tizard Learning Disability Review*, Vol. 2, No. 2, pp. 6–14

Beyer, S. and Kilsby, M. (1996b) The future of employment for people with learning disabilities: a keynote review. *British Journal of Learning Disabilities* 24: 134-137

Bignall, T., Butt, J. and Pagarani, D. (2002) *'Something To Do': The Development of Peer Support Groups for Young Black and Minority Ethnic Disabled and Deaf People*, York: The Policy Press

Boyle, J. Crichton, R. and Wellier, C. (2003) *Developing Post-school Psychological Services: Interim Report*, Edinburgh: Scottish Executive

Burchardt, T. (2005) *The Education and Employment of Disabled Young People: Frustrated Ambition*, York: The Policy Press

Cattermole, M., Jahoda, A. and Markova, I. (1990) 'Quality of life for people with learning difficulties moving to community homes', *Disability, Handicap and Society*, Vol. 5, No. 2, pp. 137–52

Chappell, A. L. (1992) 'Towards a sociological critique of the normalisation principle', *Disability and Society*, Vol. 7, No. 1, pp. 35–51

Chappell, A. L. (1997) 'From normalisation to where?', in Barton, L. and Oliver, M. (eds) (1997) *Disability Studies: Past, Present and Future*, Leeds: Disability Press

Conners, C. and Stalker, K. (2002) *The Views and Experiences of Disabled Children and Their Siblings: A Positive Outlook*, London: Jessica Kingsley Publishers

Cook, A., Petch, A., Glendinning, C. and Glasby, J. (2007) 'Building capacity in health and social care partnerships: key messages from a multi-stakeholder network', *Journal of Integrated Care*, Vol. 15, No. 4, pp. 3–10

Corden, A. and Ellis, A. (2004) 'Volunteering and employability: exploring the link for Incapacity Benefit recipients', *Benefits*, Vol. 4, No. 12, pp. 112–18

Corden, A., Harries, T., Hill, K., Kellard, K., Lewis, J., Sainsbury, R. and Thornton, P. (2003)

New Deal for Disabled People National Extension: Findings from the First Wave of Qualitative Research with Clients, Job Brokers and Jobcentre Plus Staff, Sheffield: Department of Work and Pensions

Curtice, L. (2006) *How's It Going? A Survey of What Matters Most to People with Learning Disabilities in Scotland Today*, Glasgow: Enable Scotland

Curtice, L. and Long, L. (2002) 'The health log: developing a health monitoring tool for people with learning disabilities within a community support agency', *British Journal of Learning Disabilities*, Vol. 30, No. 2, pp. 68–72

Curtice, L., Collacott, D., Espie, C., Ibbotson, T., Long, L., Morrison, J., Ayana, M. and MacIntyre, G. (2001a) *Whose Responsibility? The Health Needs of People with Learning Disabilities Living in the Community*, Edinburgh: Chief Scientist Office

Curtice, L., Collacott, D., Espie, C., Ibbotson, T., Long, L., Morrison, J., Cooper, S. A., Watkins, J. and MacIntyre, G. (2001b) *An Evaluation of a Health Check Instrument for People with Learning Disabilities in Greater Glasgow*, final report to Greater Glasgow NHS Board, Glasgow: Greater Glasgow NHS Board

Davey, V., Fernández, J., Knapp, M., Vick, N., Jolly, D., Swift, P., Tobin, R., Kendall, J., Ferrie, J., Pearson, C., Mercer, G. and Priestley, M. (2007) *Direct Payments: A National Survey of Direct Payments Policy and Practice*, London: Personal Social Services Research Unit

Department for Education and Skills (2001) *Special Educational Needs: Code of Practice*, Nottinghamshire: DfES Publications

Department for Education and Skills (2002) *Classification of Special Educational Needs: Consultation Document*, LEA/0462/2002, London: DfES

Department for Education and Skills (2005) *Youth Matters*, London: Her Majesty's Stationery Office

Department for Work and Pensions (2002) *Pathways to Work: Helping Disabled People into Employment*, London: Her Majesty's Stationery Office

Department for Work and Pensions (2006) *A New Deal for Welfare: Empowering People to Work*, London: Her Majesty's Stationery Office

Department for Work and Pensions (2007) *In Work, Better Off*, London: Her Majesty's Stationery Office

Department of Health (1992) *The Health of the Nation Strategy*, London: Her Majesty's Stationery Office

Department of Health (2001) *Valuing People: A New Strategy for Learning Disability for the 21st Century*, London: Her Majesty's Stationery Office

Department of Social Security (1998) *New Ambitions for Our Country: A New Contract for Welfare*, London: Her Majesty's Stationery Office

Diesfield, K. (1999) 'International ethical safeguards: genetics and people with learning disabilities', *Disability and Society*, Vol. 14, No. 1, pp. 21–36

Drake, R. (2000) 'Disabled people, New Labour, benefits and work', *Critical Social Policy*, Vol. 20, No. 4, pp. 421–30

Duffy, S. (2003) *Keys to Citizenship*, Liverpool: Paradigm

Finkelstein, V. (1981) *Attitudes and Disabled People: Issues for Discussion*, New York: World Rehabilitation Fund

Forrester-Jones, R., Carpenter, J., Cambridge, P., Tate, A., Hallam, A., Knapp, M. and Beecham, J. (2002) 'The quality of life of people 12 years after resettlement from long stay hospitals: users' views on their living environment, daily activities and future aspirations', *Disability and Society*, Vol. 17, No. 7, pp. 741–58

Giddens, A. (1998) *The Third Way: The Renewal of Social Democracy*, Cambridge: Polity Press

Glasgow City Council (2000) *Glasgow City Joint Community Care Plan, 2001–2004*, Glasgow: Glasgow City Council

Glasgow City Council (2001) *Glasgow's School Leavers 2000-2001*. Glasgow: The Printing Works

Glasgow City Council (2003) *Equal Access to Employment: Consultation Document*,

Glasgow: Glasgow City Council
Gooding, C. (2003) 'The Disability Discrimination Act: winners and losers', paper to the Working Futures: Disability and Work Seminar, University of Sunderland, 3 December 2003
Goodley, D. (2001a) 'Learning difficulties, the social model of disability and impairment: challenging epistemologies', *Disability and Society*, Vol. 16, No. 2, pp. 207–31
Goodley, D. (2001b) 'Against a politics of victimisation: disability, culture and self-advocates with learning difficulties', in Riddell, S. and Watson, N. (eds) (2001) *Disability, Culture and Identity*, Harlow: Pearson Education
Gosling, V. and Cotterill, L. (2000) 'An employment project as a route to social inclusion for people with learning difficulties?', *Disability and Society*, Vol. 15, No. 7, pp. 1001–18
Hales, G. (ed.) (1996) *Beyond Disability: Towards an Enabling Society*, London: Sage
Harris, J. (2002) 'Caring for citizenship', *British Journal of Social Work*, Vol. 32, No. 3, pp. 267–81
Hasler, E. and Stewart, A. (2004) *Making Direct Payments Work: Identifying and Overcoming Barriers to Implementation*, Brighton: Pavilion Publishing
Hendey, N. and Pascall, G. (2002) 'Disability and transition to adulthood: achieving independent living', paper given to Young People 2002: Research, Practice and Policy Conference, University of Keele, 22–24 July 2002
Heywood, F. and Turner, L. (2007) *Better Outcomes, Lower Costs: Implications for Health* and *Social Care Budgets of Investment in Housing Adaptations, Improvements* and *Equipment: A Review of the Evidence*, London: Her Majesty's Stationery Office
Higgins, E., Raskind, M. H., Goldberg, R. J. and Herman, K. L. (2002) 'Stages of acceptance of a learning disability: the impact of labelling', *Learning Disability Quarterly*, Vol. 25, No. 1, pp. 3–18
Hirst, M. and Baldwin, S. (1994) *Unequal Opportunities: Growing Up Disabled*, London: Social Policy Research Unit
Ho, A. (2004) 'To be labelled, or not to be labelled: that is the question', *British Journal of Learning Disabilities*, Vol. 32, No. 2, pp. 86–92
Howison, C. (2003) *Destination of Early Leavers: Evidence from the Scottish School Leavers Survey*, Special Centre for Educational Research Briefing Number 28. Edinburgh: Centre for Educational Research
Hudson, B. (2007) 'What lies ahead for partnership working? Collaborative contexts and policy tensions', *Journal of Integrated Care*, Vol. 10, No. 3, pp. 29–36
Huxley, P. (2001) 'Work and mental health: an introduction to the special section', *Journal of Mental Health*, Vol. 10, No. 4, pp. 367–72
Hyde, M. (1998) 'Sheltered and supported employment in the 1990s:the experience of disabled workers in the UK', *Disability and Society*, Vol.15, No. 2, pp. 327–41
Hyde, M. (2000) 'From welfare to work? Social policy for disabled people of working age in the UK in the 1990s', *Disability and Society*, Vol. 15, No. 2, pp. 327–41
Johnston, L., MacDonald, R., Mason, P., Riddell, L. and Webster, C. (2000) *Snakes and Ladders: Young People, Transition and Social Exclusion*, Bristol: The Policy Press
Jolly, D. (2000) 'A critical evaluation of the contradictions for the disabled worker arising from the emergence of the flexible labour market in Britain', *Disability and Society*, Vol. 15, No. 5, pp. 795–810
Jones, G. (2002) *The Youth Divide: Diverging Paths to Adulthood*, York: Joseph Rowntree Foundation
Jones, S., Morgan, J., Murphy, D. and Shearn, J. (2002) *Making It Work: Strategies for Success in Supported Employment*, Brighton: Pavilion Publishing
Kane, J., Riddell, S., Millward, A., Banks, P., Boynes, A., Dyson, A. and Wilson, A. (2003) 'Special Educational Needs and Individualised Education Plans: issues of parent and pupil participation', *Scottish Educational Review*, Vol. 35, No. 1, pp. 38–47
Kerr, M. (1998) 'Primary health care and health gain for people with a learning disability', *Tizard Learning Disability Review*, Vol. 3, No. 4, pp. 6–14
Kerr, M. (2004) 'Improving the general health of people with learning disabilities', *Advances*

in Psychiatric Treatment, Vol. 10, pp. 200–6

Klotz, J. (2001) 'Sociocultural study of intellectual disability: moving beyond labelling and social constructionist perspectives', *British Journal of Learning Disabilities*, Vol. 32, No. 2, pp. 93–104

Kregel, J. (1997) 'Supported employment', *Remedial and Special Education*, Vol. 18, No. 4, pp.194–6

Levitas, R. (2004) 'Lets hear it for Humpty: social exclusion, the third way and cultural capital', *Cultural Trends*, Vol. 13, No. 2, pp. 41–56

Lund, B. (1999) '"Ask not what your community can do for you": obligations, New Labour and welfare reform', *Critical Social Policy*, Vol. 19, No. 4, pp. 447–62

Mabbett, D. (2005) 'Some are more equal than others: definitions of disability in social policy and discrimination law', *Journal of Social Policy*, Vol. 34, No. 2, pp. 215–33

Mank, D., Cioffi, A. and Yovanoff, P. (1997) 'Analysis of the typicalness of supported employment jobs, natural supports and wage and integration outcomes', *Mental Retardation*, Vol. 35, No. 3, pp. 185–97

Marshall, T. H. (1981) *The Right to Welfare*, London: Heinemann

Martin, D. M., Roy, A. and Wells, M. B. (1997) 'Health gain through health checks: improving access to primary health care for people with intellectual disability', *Journal of Intellectual Disability Research*, Vol. 41, No. 5, pp. 401–8

May, D. and Simpson, M. K. (2003) 'The parent trap: marriage, parenthood and adulthood for people with intellectual disabilities', *Critical Social Policy*, Vol. 23, No. 1, pp. 25–43

McGregor, A., Macdougall, L., Glass, A., Higgins, K., Hirst, A. and Sutherland, V. (2003) *The Glasgow Challenge*, final report. Glasgow: University of Glasgow, Training and Employment Research Unit

Meagre, N. (2003) 'Disabled people and the labour market: has the Disability Discrimination Act made a difference?', paper to the Working Futures: Disability and Work Seminar, University of Sunderland, 3 December 2003

Millward, A., Riddell, S., Banks, P., Baynes, A., Dyson, A., Kane, J. and Wilson, A. (2002) 'An investigation of Individualised Education Programmes: Part 2 – Raising the attainment of pupils with Special Educational Needs', *Journal of Research in Special Educational Needs*, Vol. 2, No. 3, pp. 1–11

Mitchell, W. (1999) 'Leaving special school: the next step and future aspirations', *Disability and Society*, Vol. 14, No. 3, pp. 753–69

Morris, J. (1991) *Pride against Prejudice: Transforming Attitudes to Disability*, London: Women's Press

Morris, J. (1999) *Hurtling into a Void: Transition to Adulthood for Young People with Complex Health and Support Needs*, Brighton: Pavilion Publishing

Morris, J. (2002) *Moving into Adulthood: Young Disabled People Moving into Adulthood*, Foundations, York: Joseph Rowntree Foundation

NHS Health Scotland (2004) *Health Needs Assessment Project: People with Learning Disabilities in Scotland*, Glasgow: NHS Health Scotland

Northway, R. (1997) 'Integration and inclusion: illusion or progress in services for disabled people?', *Social Policy and Administration*, Vol. 31, No. 2, pp. 157–72

O'Bryan, A., Simons, K., Beyer, S. and Grove, B. (2000) *A Framework for Supported Employment*, York: Joseph Rowntree Foundation

Oliver, M. (1990) *The Politics of Disablement*, Basingstoke: Macmillan

Oliver, M. (1996) *Understanding Disability: From Theory to Practice*, Basingstoke: Palgrave Press

Orme, J. (2002) 'Social work: gender, care and justice', *British Journal of Social Work*, Vol. 32, No. 6, pp. 799–814

Parent, W., Kregel, J., Wehman, P. and Metzler, H. (1991) 'Measuring the social integration of supported employment workers', *Journal of Vocational Rehabilitation*, Vol. 1, No. 1, pp. 35–49

Pascall, G. and Hendey, N. (2002) *Disability and Transition to Adulthood: Achieving Independent Living*, Bristol: Pavilion Publishing

Pearson, C. (ed.) (2006) *Direct Payments and Personalisation of Care*, Edinburgh: Dunedin Academic Press

Petch, A., Rosengard, A., Naumann, L. and Dean, J.(2000) '*"Help Me Out, Let Me In"*: *Reprovisioning, Resettlement and the Scope for Social Inclusion in Scotland, Volume 2*, Edinburgh: Scottish Homes

Pitt, V. and Curtin, M. (2004) 'Integration versus segregation: the experiences of a group of disabled students moving from mainstream school into special needs further education', *Disability and Society*, Vol. 19, No. 4, pp. 352–61

Raffe, D. (2003) *Young People Not in Education, Employment or Training*, Centre for Educational Studies (CES) Special Briefing Paper, Edinburgh: Centre for Educational Studies

Reindal, S. M. (1999) 'Independence, dependence, interdependence: some reflections on the subject and personal autonomy', *Disability and Society*, Vol. 14, No. 3, 353–67

Riddell, S. (2004) 'The classification of pupils at the educational margins in Scotland: shifting categories and frameworks. Issues in the classification of students with disabilities revisited: perspectives and purposes of disability classification systems', paper to the Third Anglo-American Symposium on Special Education and School Reform, June 2004

Riddell, S. and Banks, P. (2001) *Disability in Scotland: A Baseline Study*, Edinburgh: Disability Rights Commission

Riddell, S., Wilson, A. and Baron, S. (1999) 'Supported employment in Scotland: theory and practice', *Journal of Vocational Rehabilitation*, Vol. 12, No. 3, p. 181–94

Riddell, S., Adler, M., Mordaunt, E. and Farmakopoulou, N. (2000) 'Special educational needs and competing policy frameworks in England and Scotland', *Journal of Educational Policy*, Vol. 15, No. 6, pp. 621–35

Riddell, S., Baron, S. and Wilson, A. (2001) *The Learning Society and People with Learning Difficulties*, Bristol: The Policy Press

Riddell, S., Wilson, A., Adler, M. and Mordaunt, E. (2002) 'Parents, professionals, and special educational needs policy frameworks in England and Scotland', *Policy and Politics*, Vol. 30, No. 3, pp. 411–25

Riddell, S., Banks, P. and Thornton, P. (2003) 'Disabled people, employment and the work preparation scheme', paper to the Working Futures: Disabled People and Work Seminar, University of Sunderland, 3 December 2003

Riddell, S., Tinklin, T. and Banks, P. (2005) *Disability and Employment in Scotland: A Review of the Evidence Base, Research Findings No. 15/2005*, Edinburgh: Scottish Executive Social Research

Riddell, S., Pearson, C., Barnes, C., Jolly, D., Mercer, G. and Priestly, M. (2006) 'The development of direct payments in the UK: the implications for social justice', *Social Policy and Society*, Vol. 4, No. 1, pp. 75–85

Roulstone, A. (2002) 'Disabling pasts, enabling futures? How does the changing nature of capitalism impact on the disabled worker and job-seeker?', *Disability and Society*, Vol. 17, No. 6, pp. 627–42

Roulstone, A., Gradwell, L., Price, J. and Child, L. (2002) *Thriving and Surviving at Work: Disabled People's Employment Strategies*, Brighton: The Policy Press

Roulstone, A. (2003) 'The legal road to rights? Disability, premises, obiter dicta, and the Disability Discrimination Act 1995', *Disability and Society*, Vol. 18, No. 2, pp.117–31

Royal College of Nursing (2006) *Meeting the Health Needs of People with Learning Disabilities: Guidance for Nursing Staff*, London: Royal College of Nursing

Rummery, K. (2006) 'Disabled citizens and social exclusion: the role of direct payments', *Policy and Politics*, Vol. 34, No. 4; pp. 633–50

Sapey, B. (2000) 'Disablement in the informational age', *Disability and Society*, Vol. 15, No. 4, pp. 619–36

Schneider, J. (1998a) 'Models of specialist employment for people with mental health problems', *Health and Social Care in the Community*, Vol. 6, No. 2, pp. 120–9

Schneider, J. (1998b) 'Work interventions in mental health care: some arguments and recent evidence', *Journal of Mental Health*, Vol. 7, No. 1, pp. 81–94

Schneider, J., Simons, K. and Everatt, G. (2001) 'Impact of the national minimum wage on disabled people', *Disability and Society*, Vol. 16, No. 5, pp. 723–47

Scottish Executive (no date) 'Social Inclusion: Introduction', available at URL: www.scotland.gov.uk/Topics/People/Social-Inclusion (accessed 31 January 2008)

Scottish Executive (1998) *Opportunity Scotland*, Edinburgh: The Stationery Office

Scottish Executive (1999a) *Implementing Inclusiveness: Realising Potential: Recommendations of the Beattie Committee*, Edinburgh: The Stationery Office

Scottish Executive (1999b) *Towards a Healthier Scotland*, Edinburgh: The Stationery Office

Scottish Executive (2000a) *The Same As You? Review of Learning Disability Services in Scotland*, Edinburgh: The Stationery Office

Scottish Executive (2000b) *A Smart Successful Scotland: Ambitions for the Enterprise Networks*, Edinburgh: The Stationery Office

Scottish Executive (2002) *Local Area Co-ordination: Report of the Short Life Working Group on Local Area Co-ordination, The Same As You? National Implementation Team*, Edinburgh: The Stationery Office

Scottish Executive (2003a) *Working for a Change? Report of the Short Life Working Group on Employment, The Same As You? National Implementation Team*, Edinburgh: The Stationery Office

Scottish Executive (2003b) *Moving Forward! Additional Support for Learning*, Edinburgh: The Stationery Office

Scottish Executive (2003c) *Education (Additional Support for Learning) Bill*, Edinburgh: The Stationery Office

Scottish Executive (2003d) *A National Evaluation of the Inclusiveness Projects: Interim Report to Scottish Executive Enterprise and Lifelong Learning Department*, Edinburgh: Scottish Executive

Scottish Executive (2003e) *Measuring Progress towards a Smart Successful Scotland*, Edinburgh: The Stationery Office

Scottish Executive (2003f) *Inclusiveness – Being Implemented: Potential – Being Realised: The Beattie National Action Group Progress Report and Future Priorities*, Edinburgh: The Stationery Office

Scottish Executive (2003g) *Supported Employment for Young People Project: Scoping Exercise to Scottish Executive Enterprise, Transport and Lifelong Learning Department*, Edinburgh: Scottish Executive

Scottish Executive (2003h) *Promoting Health, Supporting Inclusion: The National Review of the Contribution of All Nurses and Midwives to the Care and Support of People with Learning Disabilities*, Edinburgh: The Stationery Office

Scottish Executive (2004) *Home At Last? The Same As You? National Implementation Group Report of the Short Life Working Group on Hospital Closure and Service Reprovision*, Edinburgh: The Stationery Office

Scottish Executive (2004b) *Closing the Opportunity Gap*, Edinburgh: The Stationery Office

Scottish Executive (2005a) *Statistics Release: Adults with Learning Disabilities, Implementation of 'The Same As You?', Scotland 2004*, Edinburgh: Scottish Executive National Statistics

Scottish Executive (2005b) *Statutory Guidance Relating to the Education (Additional Support for Learning) (Scotland) Act 2004*, Edinburgh: The Stationery Office

Scottish Executive (2005c) *Beattie Inclusiveness Projects, Final Evaluation November 2004*, Edinburgh: The Stationery Office

Scottish Executive (2005d) *Supported Employment for Young People Pilots*, Edinburgh: The Stationery Office

Scottish Executive (2005e) *Evaluation of the All Age Guidance Projects*, Edinburgh: The Stationery Office

Scottish Executive (2005f) *Literature Review of the NEET Group*, Edinburgh: The Stationery Office

Scottish Executive, (2006a) *Make My Day! The Same As You? National Implementation Group: Report of the Day Services Sub Group*, Edinburgh: The Stationery Office

Scottish Executive (2006b) *Having Your Say? The Same As You? National Implementation Group: Report of the Advocacy Sub Group*, Edinburgh: The Stationery Office

Scottish Executive (2006c) *Destinations of Leavers from Scottish Schools: 2005-06*, Edinburgh: Scottish Executive National Statistics

Scottish Executive (2006d) *Changing Lives: Report of the 21st Century Social Work Review*, Edinburgh: The Stationery Office

Scottish Executive (2007a) *Statistics Release: Adults with Learning Disabilities, Implementation of 'The Same As You?', Scotland 2006*, Edinburgh: Scottish Executive National Statistics

Scottish Executive (2007b) *National Guidance on Self Directed Support*, Scottish Government Circular CCD7/2007, Edinburgh, The Stationery Office

Scottish Executive (2007c) *Statistics Release: Direct Payments, Scotland 2007*, Edinburgh: Scottish Executive National Statistics

Select Committee on Work and Pensions (2003) *Employment for All: Interim Report*, London: Her Majesty's Stationery Office

Shakespeare, T. (ed.) (1998) *The Disability Reader: Social Science Perspectives*, London: Cassells

Shakespeare, T. and Watson, N. (1997) 'Defending the social model', *Disability and Society*, Vol. 12, No. 2, pp. 293–300

Shearn, J., Beyer, S. and Felce, D. (2000) 'The cost-effectiveness of supported employment for people with severe intellectual disabilities and high support needs: a pilot study', *Journal of Applied Research in Intellectual Disabilities*, Vol. 13, No. 1, pp. 29–37

Smyth, M. and McConkey, R. (2003) 'Future aspirations of students with severe learning disabilities and of their parents on leaving special school', *British Journal of Learning Disability*, Vol. 31, No. 1, pp. 54–59

Stafford, B. (2003) 'New deal for disabled people: an appraisal', paper for the Working Futures: Disability and Work Seminar, University of Sunderland, 3 December 2003

Stalker, K. (2002) *Young Disabled People Moving into Adulthood in Scotland*, Foundations. York: Joseph Rowntree Foundation

Stalker, K. and Hunter, S. (1999) 'To Close or Not to Close? The Future of Learning Disability Hospitals in Scotland, *Critical Social Policy*, Vol. 19, No. 2, pp. 177–94

Stalker, K., Malloch, M., Barry, M. and Watson, J. (2007) *An Evaluation of the Implementation of Local Area Co-ordination in Scotland*, Edinburgh: The Stationery Office

Stanley, K. (2003) 'The missing million: a longer term vision for disabled people', paper given to the Working Futures: Disabled People and Work Seminar, University of Sunderland, 3 December, 2003

Stepney, P., Lunch, R. and Jordan, B. (1999) 'Poverty, exclusion and New Labour', *Critical Social Policy*, Vol. 19, No. 1, pp. 109–27

Stewart, A., Petch, A. and Curtice, L. (2003) 'Moving towards integrated working in health and social care in Scotland: from maze to matrix', *Journal of Interprofessional Care*, Vol. 17, No. 4, pp 335–50

Svenhuijsen, S. (2000) 'Caring in the third way: the relation between obligation, responsibility and care in third way discourse', *Critical Social Policy*, Vol. 20, No. 1, pp. 5–37

Swain, J. and French, S. (2000) 'Towards an affirmation model of disability', *Disability and Society*, Vol. 15, No. 4, pp. 569–82

Taylor, B., McGilloway, S. and Donnelly, D. (2004) 'Preparing young adults with disabilities for employment', *Health and Social Care in the Community*, Vol. 12, No. 2, pp. 93–101

Thornton, P. (2003) 'Jobcentre Plus: specialism and mainstreaming', paper to the Working Futures: Disability and Work Seminar, University of Sunderland, 3 December 2003

Turner, S. and Moss, S. (1996) 'The health needs of adults with learning disabilities and the Health of the Nation strategy', *Journal of Intellectual Disability Research*, Vol. 40, No. 5, pp. 438–50

Valuing People Support Team (2005) *The Story So Far: Valuing People – A New Strategy for Learning Disability for the 21st Century*, Bristol: Valuing People

Walmsley, J. (1991) 'Talking to top people: some issues relating to the citizenship of people with learning disabilities', *Disability, Handicap and Society*, Vol. 6, No. 3, pp. 219–31

Walsh, P. N. and Linehan, C. (1997) 'Factors influencing the integration of Irish employees with disabilities in the workplace', *Journal of Vocational Rehabilitation*, Vol. 8, No. 1, pp. 55–64

Warr, P. (1983) 'Work, jobs and unemployment', *Bulletin of the British Psychological Society*, Vol. 36, pp. 305–11

Warr, P. (1987) *Work, Unemployment and Mental Health*, Oxford: Clarendon Press

Warr, P. (1994) 'A conceptual framework for the study of work and mental health', *Work and Stress*, Vol. 8, No. 2, pp. 84–97

Watson, N. and Farmakopoulou, N. (2003) 'Motivations for entering and pathways of progression of disabled students in further education', *International Journal of Inclusive Education*, Vol. 7, No. 3, pp. 223–39

Watson, N., McKie, L., Hughes, B., Hopkins, D. and Gregory, S. (2004) '(Inter)dependence, needs and care: the potential for disability and feminist theorists to develop an emancipatory model', *Sociology*, Vol. 38, No. 2, pp. 331–50

Wehman, P. and Kregel, J. (1995) 'At the crossroads: supported employment a decade later', *Journal of the Association of People with Severe Handicaps*, Vol. 20, No. 4, pp. 286–99

Weston, J. (2002) *Choosing, Getting and Keeping a Job: A Study Of Supported Employment for People with Complex Needs*, Edinburgh: Scottish Human Services Trust

Whoriskey, M. (2003) 'Progress with learning disability hospital closures in Scotland', *Tizard Learning Disability Review*, Vol. 8, No. 1, pp. 2–9

Williams, F. (2001) 'In and beyond New Labour: towards a new political ethic of care', *Critical Social Policy*, Vol. 21, No. 4 pp. 467–93

Williams, V. (2006) 'The views and experiences of direct payment users', in Pearson, C. (ed.) (2006) *Direct Payments and Personalisation of Care*, Edinburgh: Dunedin Academic Press

Williams, V. and Holman, A. (2006) 'Direct payments and autonomy: issues for people with learning difficulties', in Leece, J. and Bornat, J. (eds) (2006) *Developments in Direct Payments*, Bristol: The Policy Press

Wilson, A. (2003) '"Real jobs", "learning difficulties" and supported employment', *Disability and Society*, Vol. 18, No. 2, pp. 99–115

Young, A. and Chesson, R. (2008) 'Determining research questions on health risks by people with learning disabilities, carers and care-workers', *British Journal of Learning Disability*, Vol. 36, No. 1, pp. 22–31

Index